A MANUAL
FOR ALTAR GUILDS

Theology, History, and Practice

ROBERT A. PICKEN

Church Publishing
19 East 34th Street
New York, NY 10016
www.churchpublishing.org

Cover design by Newgen
Typeset by Nord Compo

ISBN 978-1-64065-709-0 (hardcover)
ISBN 978-1-64065-710-6 (eBook)

Library of Congress Control Number: 2024942460

CONTENTS

For my mom, Barbara, whose vocation on the Altar Guild
inspired my priestly ministry.

FOREWORD

I arrived early to prepare myself for the funeral. A young man, whose family had been members of our community church for generations, had died suddenly and tragically. He was particularly loved by the children of the parish, and so I knew this funeral was going to be a difficult one.

Katherine, a young woman and member of the Altar Guild, was also early. I stepped into the sanctuary and found her weeping as she was setting up the altar.

"This has never been so hard," she whispered.

To my awe, the woman continued to do her work dutifully, carefully placing the chalice, water cruet, wine cruet, and other items necessary for the Eucharist on the altar. I think it was in that moment when we both realized what it really meant to be a minister of the Altar Guild. All worship is incarnational, a practice for "real life." We recognize the uniqueness of each human being in baptism. We share bread and wine, food for our journey, with all who reach out their hands. We celebrate life's joys and sorrows in milestone rituals and sacraments, reminding us that every moment is precious and filled with God's love and mercy. And we prepare the altar, treating the gifts of God made with human hands as holy, with respect and reverence. Oh, how wonderful the world would be if we all treated creation, things, and people with the respect and dignity that a member of the Church Altar Guild possesses!

This guide for our Altar Guilds by the Reverend Canon Robert Picken is more than just a checklist and manual (though you may use it for practical purposes if you wish). It's also a beautiful reflection on the nature of ministry and the gift of those who prepare our spaces and objects for worship.

Certainly, this would be a helpful gift for the head of your Guild, but I wouldn't stop there. Invite your Altar Guild members to choose this volume for a book club and reflection time! The depth of the history, theology, and spiritual reflections will make a meaningful read for a Vestry who wants to better appreciate the work of liturgy, or an adult forum, or even an Inquirers or Newcomers class.

Rob has carefully crafted a thoughtful overview of important liturgical ideas without leaving out the necessary practical and adaptable suggestions for use. One of our greatest gifts as Episcopalians is our deep understanding and appreciation for the mystery of the Incarnation, and this book will deepen your understanding and appreciation for your life of faith in God who makes Himself present among us.

The Right Reverend Kara Wagner Sherer
Bishop, Episcopal Diocese of Rochester (New York)
July 2024

INTRODUCTION

Bless, O Lord, us Thy servants as Thou didst bless Samuel who ministered to Thine High Priest Eli, and grant us so devoutly to serve at Thine Altar on earth, that we may be deemed worthy at length to worship at the golden Altar before Thy Throne in Heaven, through Jesus Christ Our Lord. Amen.[1]

We were celebrating the wedding anniversary of my great-aunt and great-uncle when my family and I attended the Divine Liturgy at St. Michael the Archangel Ukrainian Catholic Church in Frackville, Pennsylvania.

"My Gigi used to stand there," my mother said of her grandfather, pointing to the iconostasis, the screen separating the nave from the sanctuary. "He was one of the very few lay people allowed on the other side. He was the sacristan. He set up for the services and he knew everything that was happening." As Mom smiled brightly, it became clear to me where her own ministry as a member of the Altar Guild had been inspired.

As for me, my story is slightly different. "You're a sacristy rat," my mentor priest Fr. James joked once about a decade before I was ordained. He was right, of course. I had spent a lot of time during my youth in the sacristy of Grace Episcopal Church in Massapequa, New York, where my family were active members. I served regularly as an acolyte and was head acolyte for a few years. I also often shadowed my mother as she did her work on the Altar Guild, but I didn't quite mind. I learned about how to lay out vestments for the celebrant and how to prepare "the stack;" what bier candles were (and I was often charged with carrying them out because I thought it was fun) and what liturgical colors were used when. I discovered the value of

---

1. G.T.S. Sacristan's Manual. c.1920.

helping with decorating for the holy-days by staying out of the way and carrying garbage to the dumpster without being asked. And, I was probably the only third-grader at Grace Day School who knew what a piscina was! As if through some kind of liturgical osmosis, I absorbed from the clergy and lay ministers that careful preparation for worship was important, and, that it is a joy to serve at God's altar. This all laid a firm foundation which serves me to this day in my own priestly ministry.

In the Judeo-Christian tradition, as well as in all religions, the need for individuals who make ready a place for worship is as old as the worship itself. For centuries, the members of the Altar Guilds or the sacristans have made ready our places of worship, from great cathedrals to small rural churches to contemporary urban dinner churches. Often unnoticed, many faithful people have served and continue to serve week in, week out to help our congregations gather around God's table. Quietly, these hard-working fellow Christians focus on the details, visible and invisible to the average worshipper, as they live into their vocation as custodians of the sacred.

This volume is designed to be a theological, formational, and spiritual resource for the Altar Guild member more than highly detailed practical one. Peppered with Scripture and prayers, it will examine history and tradition and will discuss this role as a vocation in the life of our Church. Illustrations, definitions and general instructions will be provided, as well as a guide for special services. Lastly, coming out of the COVID-19 pandemic, we will discuss challenges and opportunities for this vital ministry.

The congregations of the Episcopal Church are richly varied in architecture, custom, tradition, style of worship, and practice. In the end, it is hoped that this general overview can be a foundational resource and guide for this ministry and adapted to meet the needs of your congregation and our changing times.

CHAPTER ONE

ALTAR GUILD
AS A VOCATION

Now there are varieties of gifts but the same Spirit, and there are varieties of services but the same Lord, and there are varieties of activities, but it is the same God who activates all of them in everyone.

(1 Cor 12:4-6)

On the morning of Holy Saturday 2005, the sacristans of the General Theological Seminary gathered in the Chapel of the Good Shepherd as had been done for generations before. Just the day before, on Good Friday, the great bronze doors were closed and locked—the chapel becoming a tomb. We were there that morning to clean and polish everything within reach and make preparations for the Great Vigil of Easter. Our liturgy professor, The Reverend James Farwell, reminded us that we had the unique privilege of being in a space closed off to much of the seminary community. We were reminded that we had been set apart by that same community to bear the responsibility of preparing this sacred space to once again be filled with songs of Easter triumph and joy.

That evening, as the scent of brass and furniture polish was replaced with the fragrant aroma of incense, and the light from the Paschal Candle and the congregational tapers glistened off the freshly cleaned silver and marble, I learned what a gift it is to care for and make ready the sanctuary for the community who will gather to give praise to God. Even more than a gift: a vocation.

The word *vocation* is carefully chosen. The word itself comes from the Latin word *vocare*, meaning "to call" or "to summon." In the secular world, vocation has come to be used for a wide range of roles and occupations, including teaching, healthcare, business, and arts. The belief is that whatever the profession, one can fulfill a higher purpose in one's life.

In the Church, a vocation is a like a mask for God, to paraphrase Martin Luther. Through our work—secular or sacred, ordained or lay—we can see God at work. Unfortunately, the word vocation is often used solely for those who are ordained. Christian tradition and history, however, show us that vocation is not limited to ordained clergy or religious professionals; it extends to all believers.

St. Paul reminds us that the Holy Spirit inspires us in our different ministries, services, or activities based on our unique God-given gifts and talents. In his letter to the Romans, Paul discusses the diversity of gifts within the body of Christ and encourages believers to use their gifts faithfully. He lists various gifts—prophecy, service, teaching, exhortation, leadership, mercy—and emphasizes that each believer should use their gifts according to the grace given to them, with sincerity and diligence.

While the early Church did have ordained leaders, such as bishops and deacons, the concept of vocation extended beyond these formal ecclesiastical roles. All believers were called to serve one another in love and to minister to the needs of others, both within the Church and in the broader community. This would involve acts of charity, hospitality, evangelism, teaching, and prayer. The early Christians recognized the value and dignity of ordinary work and daily life as ways to live out one's vocation. Whether as farmers, artisans, merchants, or laborers, believers were encouraged to conduct themselves with honesty and compassion, bearing witness to Christ in their workplaces and communities.

In times of persecution, vocation took on a particularly poignant meaning as believers were called to bear witness to their faith, even at the cost of their lives. Martyrdom was seen as the ultimate expression of fidelity to Christ and commitment to the gospel, inspiring others to stand firm in their own vocation as followers of Jesus.

As the institutional Church expanded and Christianity dominated spiritual and civic life in Europe during the early Middle Ages, the central understanding of vocation became closely tied to religious life. This included vocations to ordained ministry, as well as lay religious orders and monastic communities. At the same time, it should be noted that within urban centers, guilds played a significant role in organizing and regulating various professions and crafts. Membership in a guild provided individuals with a sense of belonging and identity within their trade, as well as opportunities for training, apprenticeship, and economic security—similar to a Christian monastic community. Guild members saw their craft as a vocation, often imbuing their work with religious symbolism and dedication to a patron saint.

> A cobbler, a smith, a peasant—each has the work and office of his trade, and yet they are all alike consecrated priests and bishops. Further, everyone must benefit and serve every other by means of his own work or office so that in this way many kinds of work may be done for the bodily and spiritual welfare of the community, just as all the members of the body serve one another.[1]

During the Reformation, the concept of vocation underwent significant reinterpretation, particularly within the context of the Protestant movement led by figures such as Martin Luther, John Calvin, and others. A central tenet of the Protestant Reformation was the idea of the "priesthood of all believers." Reformers emphasized that all Christians, not just ordained clergy, were called to serve God and minister to others. This democratization of vocation also

---

1. "An Open Letter to The Christian Nobility of the German Nation Concerning the Reform of the Christian Estate," 1520. Introduction and Translation by C.M. Jacobs. Works of Martin Luther: With Introductions and Notes, Volume II. (Philadephia: A.J. Holman Company, 1915) at https://web.stanford.edu/~jsabol/certainty/readings /Luther-ChristianNobility.pdf

challenged the hierarchical structure of the Church and empowered lay people to play a more active role in the life of the Church.

Q. Who are the ministers of the Church?

A. The ministers of the Church are lay persons, bishops, priests, and deacons.

Q. What is the ministry of the laity?

A. The ministry of lay persons is to represent Christ and his Church; to bear witness to him wherever they may be; and, according to the gifts given them, to carry on Christ's work of reconciliation in the world; and to take their place in the life, worship, and governance of the Church.[855]

Rooted in scripture, tradition, and reason, Anglican theology affirms the priesthood of all believers and recognizes the importance of discerning and responding to God's call in a variety of ways. Ordained people—deacons, priests, and bishops—along with those in religious orders are called by God and set apart by the Church for specific ministries. Lay people are also called to exercise their gifts and talents in service to the Church and the world. Lay ministry may involve various roles, such as readers, lay preachers, Eucharistic ministers, pastoral visitors, worship leaders, and members of church committees and councils. Plenty of faithful lay people have been called from within our communities, or summoned to them, to play vital roles using their God-given skills: musicians, catechists, missionaries, counselors, administrators, and so on.

Serving at the Altar of God is an ancient ministry to which some Christians are specifically called. Understanding this ministry as a calling from God and the community should add a level of sacredness to what can otherwise be seen as merely accomplishing necessary tasks on a checklist.

The Altar Guild, or Sacristans' Guild, is a dedicated, often unsung group of individuals within the Church who play a crucial role in ensuring that the sacred space where believers gather is both maintained with dignity and prepared for liturgy. It is a practical ministry in many ways; certain vessels and vestments are needed for worship. At the same time, it is a holy ministry and one that is deeply engaged in the symbolic and the ritual and through which the Divine is encountered.

At its heart, the Altar Guild is a ministry of service. Those called to this vocation often express a deep love for the Church and a desire to contribute to the well-being of the community. While their work is usually behind the scenes, the impact of their work is felt and seen by all who enter the church or worship space. Through their attention to detail and symbolism and their commitment to service to the community, the Altar Guild contributes significantly to the congregation, making their vocation an integral one in the life of the Church today.

Almighty God our heavenly Father, you declare your glory and show forth your handiwork in the heavens and in the earth: Deliver us in our various occupations from the service of self alone, that we may do the work you give us to do in truth and beauty and for the common good; for the sake of him who came among us as one who serves, your Son Jesus Christ our Lord, who lives and reigns with you and the Holy Spirit, one God, for ever and ever. Amen. [261]

CHAPTER TWO

THE MINISTRY IN SCRIPTURE AND TRADITION

That I may go to the altar of God, to the God of my joy and gladness.

(Psalm 43:4a)

The role of the today's Altar Guild has a rich history deeply rooted in both biblical teachings and centuries-old practices. As caretakers of the sacred, their ministry connects the contemporary role to a lineage of service that spans millennia.

In ancient Israelite religious practices, the priests—descendants of Aaron—were primarily focused on offering sacrifices and leading worship. Temple Servants are also mentioned as individuals who served in various capacities within the Temple, assisting the priests and Levites in their duties. While their specific roles aren't always detailed, they likely would have been involved in tasks related to the organization and preparation of religious ceremonies, which aligns with the duties of sacristans. In the meticulous accounts about the Ark of the Covenant, individuals were assigned to carry and care for it. For example, in the Book of Numbers, specific instructions are given regarding the transport and handling of the Ark, indicating that certain individuals were designated for this responsibility. The Levites played a significant role in the administration and maintenance of the Tabernacle (and later the Temple in Jerusalem). They were responsible for various tasks related to the worship rituals, including caring for the sacred vessels, maintaining cleanliness, and assisting the priests in their duties.

Of course, the word "sacristan" is never used. However, the concept of an Altar Guild can be traced back to the Old Testament. *First Chronicles* provides an example of how the Levites assisted the priests:

> Their duty shall be to assist the descendants of Aaron for the service of the house of the Lord, having the care of the courts and the chambers, the cleansing of all that is holy, and any work for the service of the house of God; to assist also with the rows of bread, the choice flour for the grain offering, the wafers of unleavened bread, the baked offering, the offering mixed with oil, and all measures of quantity or size. And they shall stand every morning thanking and praising the Lord, and likewise at evening, and whenever burnt offerings are offered to the Lord on Sabbaths, new moons, and appointed festivals, according to the number required of them, regularly before the LORD. Thus they shall keep charge of the tent of meeting and the sanctuary and shall attend the descendants of Aaron, their kindred, for the service of the house of the Lord. (1 Chronicles 23:28-32)

Written approximately during the 4th century BCE, Chronicles is historical literature of the Hebrew Bible. In this chapter, the author details the practices of the Second Temple Period, which spanned six centuries from 516-70 BCE. The author builds on the meticulous instructions detailed in the book of Exodus given to these leaders regarding the preparation, handling, and consecration of sacred objects used in worship. In the worship customs of ancient Israel, the vestments, vessels, and incense were not only items of reverence but also tangible expressions of the people's connection with God. The same could be said today.

Centuries later, early Christian communities adopted and adapted the practices of Judaism. As the Christian Church emerged and evolved, the tradition of setting apart those responsible for the care and preparation of worship continued, if not in a formal way to start.

Day by day, as they spent much time together in the temple, they broke bread from house to house and ate their food with glad and generous hearts, praising God and having the goodwill of all the people. And day by day the Lord added to their number those who were being saved. (Acts 2:46-47)

The Book of Acts describes how the first Christians met together for the breaking of bread—which describes both the sharing of a meal and the Lord's Supper. (We will discuss this again when we discuss contemporary dinner churches.) Again while the term "sacristan" as we understand it in later Christian traditions may not have been used in these contexts, there were certainly individuals who undertook similar roles in facilitating worship within these house churches. The owners of the house where the Church gathered would have played a central role as hosts in providing the space for prayer and worship, seating and gathering space for the attendees, and often food and drink for communal meals that might accompany these gatherings. Prisca and Aquila are prime examples of this ministry of hospitality and service as we see in the Acts of the Apostles and also Paul's writings (Rom 16:3-4; 1 Cor 16:19). They are commemorated on our church calendar on July 8.

Following the legalization of the religion in the Roman Empire in 313 CE and then the expansion following Christianity being declared the official religion in 380 CE, the Church needed to move from meeting in homes of fellow Christians to larger central gathering spaces. Obviously, a dedicated corps of individuals responsible for preparation for worship was necessary. This is also the time when the expansion of the role and responsibilities of the presbyterate was taking place and many of the functions that once fell to hosts in house churches transferred to the ordained priests.

By the early Middle Ages, the formalization of the sacristan's role was well underway within the Church structure. Pope Gregory IX writes about the sacristan as an honorable office responsible for the maintenance of vestments, sacred vessels, and lights; again, these were often priests, especially in cathedrals. Monastic communities, in particular, emphasized the importance of ritual and order, with sacristans taking on a prominent position in maintaining chapels and oratories. Their duties extended beyond the Eucharist to include the coordination of liturgical events, care for vestments, and the overall upkeep of the worship space.

During the Protestant Reformation, the role of a sacristan underwent significant changes in many parts of Europe. As reformers sought to simplify church rituals and remove what they viewed as vain and popish superstition and as non-biblical practices, sacristans found themselves at the center of religious upheaval. In some cases, monasteries were destroyed, and cathedrals and parish churches were stripped of vestments and sacred vessels. Protestant leaders often abolished or minimized the use of elaborate vestments, ceremonial objects, and rituals. Thus, the role of the sacristan evolved or, in some cases, disappeared altogether.

The Making of a Modern Altar Guild

The Oxford Movement, also known as the Tractarian Movement, was a significant religious and intellectual movement within the Church of England in the 19th century. It emerged as a response to perceived theological and liturgical deficiencies within Anglicanism, seeking to revitalize and restore the Church's connection to its Catholic roots. Led by prominent figures such as John Henry Newman, John Keble, and Edward Bouverie Pusey, the movement took its name from the university city where its leaders were based.

At its core, the Oxford Movement aimed to counter what its proponents saw as the erosion of traditional doctrine and practice within the Church of England. They argued for a return to the principles of sacramental worship, apostolic succession, and the authority of the Church Fathers. Central to their mission was the promotion of a High-Church theology that emphasized the importance of liturgy.

One of the key strategies employed by the Oxford Movement was the publication of the "Tracts for the Times," a series of pamphlets that expounded its theological positions and critiques of contemporary Anglicanism. These tracts sparked widespread debate and controversy within the Church, leading to both condemnation and support from various quarters.

Although the Oxford Movement did not achieve all of its objectives, its impact on the Church of England and broader Anglicanism was profound. It helped to reinvigorate theological discourse, inspire a revival of ritualism and sacramentalism, and establish the groundwork for the broader liturgical movement that would develop in the late 19th and early 20th centuries.

Because of this movement, sacristans resumed their significant role in the life of the Church with the reintroduction of ceremonial vestments and incense, the weekly if not daily celebration of the Eucharist, and other ritual practices and elaborate customaries. Sacristans once again became essential figures.

At this time in the Episcopal Church, Altar Guilds were formed and evolved in response to changing theological, liturgical, and social currents These new Altar Guilds operated within the broader context of the liturgical movement described above. As the use of vestments and altar paraments, candles, flowers, and other decorations became more and more common practice, Altar Guilds needed to become larger, more structured, and formalized—drawing inspiration from medieval monasticism, whether they knew it or not.

It should be noted here that because leadership in the Church—whether ordained or in governance—was limited to men, women predominantly took on these roles (and oftentimes ran their guilds with more efficiency and effectiveness). Members were trained in the intricacies of liturgical practice, and meticulous attention was paid to the arrangement of altar linens, the care of vestments, and the preparation of the altar for Holy Communion.

The mid-to-late 20th century in the Episcopal Church saw an increased interest in liturgical renewal and the recovery of ancient Christian practices within the liturgical life of the Church. This was reflected in the work of Altar Guilds, which sought to integrate elements of the early Church's worship into contemporary liturgy. And that renewal and revision continues to this day, as we will see in coming chapters.

While specific duties may vary, the essence of the role of the Altar Guild remains consistent. The biblical and historical tradition underscores the importance of order, reverence, and meticulous care in the practice of worship. As custodians of the sacred, our Altar Guilds carry forward a legacy that spans centuries, embodying the commitment to create a space where the divine presence is honored and worship is conducted—linking the contemporary Church to our most ancient roots.

O God, you accepted the service of Levites in your temple, and your Son was pleased to accept the loving service of his friends: Bless the ministry of the Altar Guild and give them grace, that they, caring for the vessels and vestments of your worship and the adornment of your sanctuary, may make the place of your presence glorious; through Jesus Christ our Lord. Amen.[1]

---

1. *Prayers for Pastor and People.* Carlozzi, Carl, ed. (Church Publishing, New York, 1984)

CHAPTER THREE

AN INTRODUCTION
TO LITURGY

Liturgy is not something beautiful we do for God, but something beautiful God does for us and among us.[1]

Nathan D. Mitchell

There is a tale about a man who wished to marry a beautiful noblewoman; the problem was that he was a notorious villain. He had a clever idea: during the week-long festival of their village's patron saint, he would wear the mask of a saint and act like the saint to win her over. As the festivities continued, he became close with the young woman and his friends grew jealous. Wanting to reveal him as the village's villain, they waited until the couple was dancing, sneaked up to him, and removed his mask. In a dramatic turn of events, when they did so, his face had turned into the face of the saint! The once-notorious villain and the young noblewoman then lived happily ever after.[2]

This fable is a good illustration to start a chapter on the theology of worship. By donning the mask of the saint and practicing a holy life, the villain had become the saint he was pretending to be. In the same way, as we don the mask of Christ and rehearse a holy life in worship, we are transformed into who we are called to be as followers of Jesus in the world.

---

1. Mitchell, Nathan D. "The Amen Corner: Being Good and Being Beautiful," *Worship* 74, no. 6. (November 2000) in *Sacraments and Worship: The Sources of Christian Theology*. Johnson, Maxwell, ed. (Louisville: Westminster John Knox, 2012) 97.

2. I don't remember when or where I first heard this story. Credit here belongs to Farwell, James. *The Liturgy Explained*. (New York: Morehouse, 2013), 1.

"Being Christian…is not really about holding certain beliefs about God and the world, but about becoming a certain kind of person before God and in the world," explains theologian James Farwell in *The Liturgy Explained*.[3] To this point, think of the parable of the Good Samaritan in Luke's Gospel (10:30-37): a person lies beaten near to death on the side of the road; the priest and the Levite, the ancient version of the sacristan, both walk by, *believing* that God is merciful; but it is the Samaritan, the outsider, who *acts* mercifully by caring for the injured one.

Our corporate gatherings for prayer—sometimes called liturgy, service, worship, or some combination thereof—plays the primary role in our formation as Christians. Given the Altar Guild's key role in enabling and supporting public, communal prayer, it is essential to spend some time on the concept of liturgical theology.

Let's start first with defining *theology*. Theology is the philosophical discipline that studies religious belief and the nature of the Divine. The word itself comes from the Greek words *Theos*, meaning God, and *Logos*, meaning word or discourse. This millennia-old academic discipline and spiritual practice that crosses cultural and religious traditions can be summed up in the contemporary expression: God-Talk.

Liturgical theology is a narrower discipline that *talks* about God at work in our *worship*. Defining what we mean by liturgy or worship—and the nature of the Divine in relation to it—is the focus of this chapter and even then, this barely scratches the surface.

With the Altar Guild being a ministry focused on details, it would be easy for us to lose sight of the forest for the trees, as the saying goes. In other words, as is the goal of this book, it is helpful for us to look at the bigger picture.

Throughout Christian history, theologians—those who practice the discipline of theology—have written and spoken beautifully about the over-arching purpose of our worship and liturgy. Often their

---

3. Ibid, 3.

ideas overlap, but each adds new insights, creating a rich tapestry of thought about God at work in our worship.

Irenaeus was a 2nd century bishop. Born in modern-day Turkey, Irenaeus became the second Bishop of Lyon in modern-day France in about 177 CE. He is most well-known for his writings *Against Heresies*. He died in the early 3rd century and was buried under the Church of St. John in Lyon, later renamed to his honor and then destroyed by French Protestants in the 16th century. In interpreting his writings, James White notes that Irenaeus believed that "nothing glorifies God more than a human being made holy; nothing is more likely to make a person holy than their desire to glorify God."[4] Our worship, then, is about the glorification of God and the sanctification of the people.

By the early Middle Ages, Christianity had developed prescribed liturgies which were more organized and formal. Prosper of Aquitaine, a disciple of Augustine of Hippo who lived in Gaul (modern-day France), was a layman who threw himself into his vocation as a theologian. A prolific writer, he was well-known for his defense of orthodoxy—right or commonly held beliefs—against the heresy of Pelagianism, which suggested choice in human salvation rather than the universal saving action of Jesus Christ. For our purposes, Prosper is remembered for the commonly used maxim *lex orandi lex credendi*, or more accurately translated, "that the law of prayer may establish a law for belief." He wrote further, "For when the presidents of the holy congregations perform their duties, they plead the cause of the human race before the divine clemency, and joined by the sighs of the whole Church, they beg and pray" for the grace and mercy of God.[5]

Now, the role of the people became more of bystanders, who offered their private prayers and devotions—the "sighs of the whole Church," for Prosper—in the liturgies of the Church. Rooted deeply

---

4. White, James F. *Introduction to Christian Worship.* (Nashville: Abingdon Press, 200), 24.

5. Prosper of Aquitaine. *Capitula Coelestini* 8 (Migne, *Patrologia Latina* 51, 205-12), trans Geoffrey Wainwright in *Sacraments and Worship: The Sources of Christian Theology.* Johnson, Maxwell, ed. (Louisville: Westminster, 2012), 51.

in the ancient Jewish understanding of priests offering sacrifices on behalf of the people, this became the predominant understanding of worship, in Western Christianity at least, for most of the Middle Ages. After a half-millennium, this would begin to change.

> Lift up your heads, O gates; lift them high, O everlasting doors; * and the King of glory shall come in. (Psalm 24:7)

John Calvin was a leading Protestant Reformer of the 16th century. Born and educated in France, Calvin spent a good portion of his life in Geneva, Switzerland, where he was a pastor and a leading voice for reform in the Church. Today in the English-speaking world, Calvin is most associated with Presbyterianism. In his extended commentary on Psalm 24, Calvin wrote, "We are lifted up even to God by the exercises of religion. What is the design of the preaching of the Word, the sacraments, the holy assemblies, and the whole external government of the Church, but that we may be united to God?"[6]

In our Anglican tradition, we can look to Thomas Cranmer. Born in 1489, Cranmer was Archbishop of Canterbury from 1533 to 1555 under the reigns of Kings Henry VIII and Edward VI and a leader of the English Reformation. Cranmer wrote and compiled the first two editions of the Book of Common Prayer in 1549 and 1552. He was burned at the stake as a heretic during the reign of Queen Mary I in 1556. Nonetheless, Cranmer laid the foundation for our traditional belief that our worship is directed to God's glory and to our morality; this is echoed even today in modern theologies that link worship to social action and justice. For Cranmer, the purpose of worship was the "setting forth of God's honor or glory, and to the reducing[7] of the people to a most perfect and godly living."[8]

---

6. Calvin, John. "Commentary on Psalm 24:7" *Commentaries 31:248.* in White, 23.

7. For Cranmer, *reduction* should not be viewed as a demeaning, humiliating, or bringing low, but rather can be compared to the boiling down of a substance to get to its essence.

8. "Of Ceremonies," *The First and Second Prayer Book of Edward VI* (New York: Dutton, 1952), 326. Spelling modernized.

We will turn also to more contemporary writers as we continue this discussion, but with this historical picture in mind, we can begin to explore the various elements and practices that constitute Christian worship. Here it is crucial to define key terms that form the foundation of this theological discipline. In the rest of this chapter, we will delve into the meanings of essential concepts, including ritual, sacraments, worship, service, and liturgy by shedding light on their implications within the context of our Christian faith and practice.

It is best to start with fundamental building block for our liturgical practice: *ritual*. Rituals can be secular or religious, and they can serve various purposes, such as marking important life events, reinforcing social bonds, expressing beliefs, or achieving personal or collective transformation. More so than daily routines (i.e. brushing our teeth or making a pot of coffee each morning), rituals involve elements of symbolism, repetition, and formality.

Symbolism in rituals allows participants to connect the material world with the spiritual or abstract. For example, lighting a candle can symbolize bringing light into darkness, hope, or remembrance. Repetition in rituals reinforces their meaning and significance, embedding them deeply into the consciousness of participants. Formality provides a structure that differentiates ritual activities from pedestrian activities, lending them a sense of sacredness or importance.

In this way, rituals operate on multiple levels: they are performative acts that symbolize certain beliefs and values of a community, and they enact those same beliefs and values. For instance, the civic ritual of singing the national anthem expresses a shared identity and solidarity. And, the performance of the national anthem, together with the requisite standing and placing a hand over the heart, enacts a shared identity and unity of national pride and spirit among those present. (Think also about how the ritualized action of not participating in this same civic ritual can have its own power: both real and symbolic.)

In religious contexts, rituals are profoundly meaningful. They not only express and communicate the beliefs of the community but also create a space for the sacred and the divine to interact with humanity. Think of the Jewish custom of lighting Sabbath candles to usher in the day of holy rest and peace. Typically performed by women, the ritual involves kindling and blessing candles with the candle-lighter then waving their hand three times over the flames, literally drawing in the warmth of the flames to oneself and symbolically ushering in the warmth of the day's rest before offering the traditional blessing and their own private prayers. "Shabbat Shalom" is then said to the others gathered, drawing the assembly into the Sabbath peace and rest. Here symbolism, repetition, and formality combine to express the meaning of Sabbath while bringing it to reality.

Likewise, Christianity is rich in rituals that have evolved over two millennia, playing a crucial role in the faith and practice of Christians. We call these rituals *sacraments*. The sacraments, as defined by most Christian traditions, are outward and visible signs of an inward and spiritual grace. In his profound work *Symbol and Sacrament*, the great French Jesuit theologian of the 20th century, Louis-Marie Chauvet, describes them this way:

> [Sacraments] are the witnesses of a God who is never finished with coming: the amazed witnesses of a God who comes continually; the patient witnesses, patient unto weariness at times, of a God who is not here except by mode of passage. And of this passage, the sacraments are the trace...[9]

The sacraments, in other words, are our best connection to the Divine, who is continually at work in the world. In upcoming chapters, we will discuss specific sacraments in more detail; for now, it is helpful to note while sacraments are not our sole connections to God, they

---

9. Chauvet, Louis-Marie. *Symbol and Sacrament: A Sacramental Reinterpretation of Christian Existence.* Patrick Madigan and Madeline Beaumont, trans. (The Liturgical Press: Collegeville, MN, 1995), 555.

are the primary and ritualized means by which our community of believers encounter the living God to whom we offer thanksgiving and praise.

That offering of thanksgiving and praise to God is often called *worship*. Worship is a word used across the globe in virtually all religious and spiritual contexts and the concept can be traced back to the earliest records of human civilization. The word itself derives from the Old English word *weorthscipe*, which combines *weorth* meaning "value," and *scipe* meaning "condition." Thus, it conveys the idea of assigning value to something or someone—in our case, God.

Throughout Scripture, the English term "worship" can be used to describe acts of reverence, adoration, and devotion directed towards God. In the Old Testament, Hebrew words such as *shachah* (to bow down) and *abad* (to serve) convey the physical and spiritual aspects of worship. Worship involves acts of humility and service, reflecting a deep and abiding respect for God's majesty and sovereignty. Look, for example, at Psalm 95:6: "Come, let us bow down, and bend the knee, and kneel before the Lord our Maker." [725]

The Greek word *proskunein*, meaning to fall down, to show obedience, or to prostrate, is used for the worship of God frequently in the New Testament. In John's Gospel, Jesus tells the Samaritan woman at the well: "the hour is coming and is now here when the true worshipers will worship the Father in spirit and truth" (4:23). To distinguish from other religious ritual practice, *sébein*, meaning to revere, is used frequently to refer to worship of false gods (see Mark 7:7 or Acts 19:27). Finally, one other word frequently used is *latreia*, translated as both worship and service.

So, we come to the word: *service*. Here again we can see that service carries multiple layers of meaning, encompassing concepts of duty, assistance, and devotion in various contexts. Its etymology can be traced back to the Latin word *servitium*, meaning "slavery" or "in assistance to." We can turn to Jesus saying, "It is written, 'Worship the Lord your God, and serve only him.'" (Luke 4:8)

We are presented with an interesting challenge here in that our English words of worship and service could simply imply a one-sided relationship: we are obliged to offer praise to a far-off deity. A familiar hymn might begin to help provide some clarity:

O worship the King, all glorious above!

O gratefully sing his power and his love!

Our shield and defender, the Ancient of Days,

pavilioned in splendor and girded with praise.

…In thee do we trust, nor find thee to fail;

Thy mercies, how tender! How firm to the end!

Our Maker, Defender, Redeemer, and Friend![10]

We find ourselves now with the wonderful German word: *Gottesdienst.* From the German words for "God" and "service" or "work," there is no easy, direct translation into English; in fact, it takes several words to do it: God's service to us and our service to God. This reflects the God who "emptied himself, taking the form of a slave, assuming human likeness." (Philippians 2:7) This term for worship implies a mutuality in the relationship where both parties— God and God's people—are acting. God, who the hymn-writer calls "our Maker, Defender, Redeemer, and Friend," acts in a caring and loving relationship and we respond in worship and service.

Service, or *latreia,* can mean both worship in the temple or a sense of religious duty, as seen in Paul's Letter to the Romans: "I appeal to you therefore, brothers and sisters, on the basis of God's mercy, to present your bodies as a living sacrifice, holy and acceptable to God, which is your reasonable act of worship." (12:1) It would seem for Paul that there is both worship, or what our prayer book calls the "service of the sanctuary" [99], and the offering of our entire life as an act of worship and service to God. This idea of service then extends

---

10. Grant, Robert. "O worship the King." (New York: The Church Hymnal, 1985), 388.

the ethos of worship beyond the confines of sacred spaces into the fabric of everyday life. Maybe you remember the popular expression in the Episcopal Church a decade or so ago: *Our worship has ended and our service begins.*

Following the teachings of Jesus, who exemplified servanthood, Christian service encapsulates acts of compassion, justice, mercy, and love enacted in response to God's grace. Service becomes a tangible expression of one's faith, reflecting the transformative power of worship in shaping attitudes, values, and behaviors towards others. Whether through acts of charity, advocacy for justice, or ministry to the marginalized, service embodies the holistic worship of God through concrete actions that uphold the dignity and welfare of all.

Having defined ritual, sacrament, worship and service, we come to the concept of *liturgy*. Our understanding of liturgy, like our preceding terms, encompasses a rich and varied history, reflecting the dynamic interplay between tradition, cultural context, and theological development.

Derived from a Greek term, liturgy underscores the active participation of believers in the worship of God. The Greek word *Leitourgia* combines *leitos*, meaning "public," and *ergon*, meaning "work" or "service." In ancient Greece, *leitourgia* was integral to societal functioning. Wealthy citizens, or benefactors, were expected to fund and perform these public services, which often included sponsoring public work projects, religious festivals, and performances of dramatic works. Contributing to both civic pride and religious devotion, these activities were seen as a form of public service and benefaction that served the well-being and betterment of the community.

Over time, the term evolved to encompass religious rites and ceremonies. As Christianity emerged and spread within the Greco-Roman world, the term liturgy began to take on a more particular meaning. Unlike the civic-oriented work *of* and *for* the people, early Christians emphasized the sacramental life of the Church. They adopted and adapted the term to describe their communal worship practices, particularly the Eucharist

It is here in the term *liturgy* that the work of ritual, sacrament, worship, and service are most fully combined. Think back to Prosper of Aquitaine, who taught that what we pray shapes our beliefs and to Archbishop Cranmer, who said that what we pray and believe shapes our godly actions. Like the young villain, who acted a certain way only to be transformed, it is through our liturgies that God is at work transforming our lives.

A more contemporary explanation comes from Robert Taft, who was a 20th century American theologian, Jesuit priest, and archimandrite, or superior abbot, of the Ukrainian Greek Catholic Church. Taft said:

> If the Bible is the Word of God in the words of men, the liturgy is the deeds of God in the actions of those humans who would live in [God]...The purpose of baptism is to make *us* cleansing waters and healing and strengthening oil; the purpose of Eucharist is not to change bread and wine, but to change you and me; through baptism and eucharist it is *we* who are to become Christ for one another, a sign to the world that is yet to hear his name. That is what Christian liturgy is all about, because that is what Christianity is all about.[11]

Christians embark on a journey of faith that shapes hearts, nourishes souls, and embodies the timeless truths of God's redemptive love. As we have seen, our common prayer and worship—our liturgy—plays a key role in this. By understanding this, a member of the Altar Guild can look beyond the practicality of the role and, hopefully, see within their vocation a call to assist fellow Christians in the work to which we are all called.

---

11. Taft, Robert, "What Does Liturgy Do? Toward a Soteriology of Liturgical Celebration: Some Theses" in *Primary Sources of Liturgical Theology,* Dwight Vogel, ed. (Collegeville: The Liturgical Press), 143.

Grant, we beseech you, Almighty God, that the words which we have heard this day with our outward ears, may, through your grace, be so grafted inwardly in our hearts, that they may bring forth in us the fruit of good living, to the honor and praise of your Name; through Jesus Christ our Lord. Amen. [834]

CHAPTER FOUR

THE LITURGICAL SPACE

Let us build a house
Where love can dwell
and all can safely live
A place where Saints and children tell
How hearts learn to forgive.
...Let us build a house where love is found
In water, wine and wheat
A banquet hall on holy ground
Where peace and justice meet.[1]

Marty Haugen

"It was like *Aida* in a phone booth," my colleague said about a service he had just attended. With his reference to the extravagant opera composed by Giuseppe Verdi, it was easy to gather there was *a lot* thrown into that liturgy. It seemed if one hymn was called for, two would be better; if there was a moment of silence, it could be filled with another prayer, poem, speech, or anthem; and, finally, "if you didn't move for a minute or two, you ran the risk of being decorated," he added to his review of this overdone event.

James White was a leading 20th century liturgical historian who taught at Emory University, the Catholic University of America, Drew University, and, at the time of his death in 2004, he was professor emeritus of liturgical studies at Notre Dame University. In his work *Introduction to Christian Worship*, White noted, "the way space is organized reflects and shapes Christian worship."[2] In this chapter,

---

1. Haugen, Marty. "All are welcome." (New York: GIA Publications, 1994), verses 1 & 4, excerpted.

2. White, James F. *Introduction to Christian Worship.* (Nashville: Abingdon Press, 200), 83.

we will examine the centers around which our liturgy is defined, and we will discuss some practical considerations for the Altar Guild to bear in mind as they go about their work and ministry.

If there is anything to learn from this chapter, it is this: the space always wins. Just as it's ridiculous to think of "*Aida* in a phone booth," the table fellowship of a small contemporary dinner church set in nave of the Basílica de la Sagrada Família in Barcelona would also be out of place. Christian communities need places to gather to worship and, while how we pray can be very similar at times, these buildings and gathering spaces can be vastly different in size, structure, and style. White also noted, "the building helps define the meaning of worship for those gathered inside it."[3] Our buildings and worship spaces share what we understand (and possibly misunderstand) about God and about the community assembled. Thoughtful clergy and sacristans will know how to use the strengths and overcome the weakness of worship space.

Our church buildings are divided into liturgical spaces and centers that are not just functional areas but are imbued with deep theological and spiritual significance. The careful design, maintenance, and use of these spaces and centers can create a setting that fosters a deeper encounter with the Divine, a stronger sense of Christian community, and a more profound participation in the sacred mysteries of the faith.

How awesome is this place! This is none other than the house of God, and this is the gate of heaven. (Genesis 28:17)

As an acolyte as a child, I would stand before this plaque on the floor in my parish church many Sundays and feast days. I learned the line by heart early on, standing there on the threshold between the narthex and nave, waiting for the procession to begin. The liminality of that spot and that moment were not lost on me, even if I didn't have the right words to describe the feeling.

---

3. Ibid, 82

The *gathering space,* often called the narthex in our church buildings, has its roots in early Christian architecture and is where the community first comes together, informally and formally. Historically, it was a place for catechumens (those preparing for baptism) and penitents. Today, it serves as a place of welcome where worshippers can greet one another, pick up bulletins, and otherwise prepare for the service. It may also serve as a space for informal gatherings, announcements, and activities before and after the service. In sum, it symbolizes the transition from the everyday world to the sacred space of worship.

Some questions that might be important for the Altar Guild to ask itself or the larger community:

- Does this space provide an adequate sense of welcome and hospitality that might include informational displays about church activities and services, good signage, coat racks, comfortable seating, warm lighting, and aesthetically pleasing décor that reflects the congregation's identity?
- Is this space easily accessible for all, including those with disabilities, with ramps, wide doorways, and accessible restrooms?
- Has consideration been given to the various uses of the space, such as for fellowship, meetings, and receptions and is there functional seating, tables, etc., if necessary?

After moving through the gathering space, worshippers will find themselves in what is usually the largest space: the *congregational space.* This is where the community of believers assembles to participate in worship, and it should foster a sense of unity and shared purpose among the worshippers. The design of this space has varied widely throughout Christian history. Early Christians gathered in homes, standing and sitting in close quarters. With the construction of dedicated church buildings, more seats, moveable benches, and anchored pews were eventually introduced. This arrangement of seating, usually facing the liturgical centers, should facilitate participation in the liturgy and emphasize the communal nature of Christian worship, the gathering of the faithful as the Body of Christ.

Questions that percolate up for me:

- Is this space clean and well-maintained and does it have the Book of Common Prayer, hymnals, bibles, and other materials necessary for worship?
- Is the seating arranged to promote a sense of community and participation with clear sightlines of the altar, lectern and pulpit or ambo, and font?
- For holidays and special occasions, do decorations of any kind obstruct view, participation, or movement within this space?

Movement space within churches has also been shaped by architectural styles and liturgical practices. For example, in early Christian basilicas, wide aisles and open spaces facilitated processions and liturgical movement. Gothic cathedrals introduced more complex floor plans, with side aisles, transepts, and ambulatories. In the Episcopal Church, movement spaces vary greatly based architectural style and building size. What is clear, though, is that this space symbolizes the pilgrimage of the faithful and the journey of the Christian life.

Movement space is essential for the dynamic aspects of worship. It allows for formal processions of choir and clergy, the movement of ministers for liturgical actions, and the participation of the congregation in moving to the font for baptism or to the altar to share in Holy Communion.

When thinking about movement space here are some questions to consider:

- Are aisles clear and unobstructed for the movement of the congregation?

- Are there clearly defined pathways for formal processions, ensuring there is ample space for clergy, acolytes, and choir members to move without obstruction?
- Is the font placed where it can be easily accessed during baptisms?
- Are there clear and unobstructed paths for special devotions (i.e. Stations of the Cross, veneration of icons, private prayers at saint's chapel, etc.)?
- How is the movement space adapted for wedding and funeral processions?

That I may go to the altar of God, to the God of my joy and gladness; * and on the harp I will give thanks to you, O God my God. (Psalm 43:4)

Our gathering, congregational, and movement spaces speak to the relationship of the community to each other and their actions within the liturgy. While the liturgy itself involves all people, *liturgical centers* refer specifically to the main focal points of the liturgy: *Word, Font*, and *Table*.

The centrality of Scripture in Christian worship has its roots in ancient Jewish synagogue practices, where readings from the Torah and the Prophets were an integral part of the service. Early Christians, many of whom were Jewish, continued this tradition, incorporating readings from the Hebrew Scriptures along with texts that would eventually form the New Testament.

The *Word*, represented primarily by the lectern and pulpit, symbolizes God's revelation to humanity. Jesus alone is *the* Word of God (see John 1), yet the Bible is also the Word of God because it is the witness to us of God's love for humanity by our ancestors in faith. The sacred text encourages, reproves, and cajoles us. The act of preaching is closely linked since the sermon directs today's listener to the call for transformation through Christ to a life well-lived in God's grace.

This center is often elevated and positioned prominently to signify the importance of the Word of God. In some congregations, there might be a single place from which scripture is read, the Holy Gospel proclaimed, and the sermon preached: this is called an Ambo. Most of our congregations have a lectern where the scripture is read and a seperate pulpit from which the sermon is preached.

Adornment of these centers with antependium or paraments vary, of course, from congregation to congregation. (Antependium comes from Latin and means "to hang before.") Lecterns are often adorned with antependia called Bible Markers or Lectern Falls; pulpits or ambos are adorned with Pulpit Falls. These are all hangings that usually match the clergy vestments and other paraments used on the altar itself, reflecting the liturgical season. In some congregations, an ambo might be unadorned or adorned with a simple hanging that connects to the identity of the congregation or setting (e.g. the seal of the diocese for a diocesan convention).

Whatever the architectural design of your building, the reading of scripture is not merely an intellectual exercise or a recitation of historical events. The proclamation of the Word of God is a sacramental act through which we believe God speaks to the congregation.

The *Font*, used for the sacrament of holy baptism, has evolved in form and location throughout Christian history. In the early Church, baptisms were often conducted in rivers or large pools. By the 4th century, dedicated baptisteries, often separate buildings adjacent to the main church, were common. In later centuries, fonts and baptismal pools became more integrated into the Church building itself. After the Reformation, fonts became smaller and more discreetly placed, as baptism became more of a private ceremony. In contemporary churches, the font is typically located near the entrance to symbolize baptism as the entry point into the Christian faith. Today, one may find the font in a variety of locations in the Episcopal Church, reflecting a wide breadth of customs around baptism.

Whether the font is used or not during a given liturgy, as a center it represents cleansing, rebirth, and initiation into the Body of Christ. The water in the font recalls the waters of creation, the Flood, the Exodus, and ultimately, the baptism of Jesus in the Jordan River. At the font, worshippers are connected to a fundamental narrative of salvation history.

As such, the Altar Guild should keep in mind a few important points. First, a font is not an over-sized vase; decoration around (or if a custom, in) the font should consider if this decoration enhances the rich symbolism of this center. Second, if holy water is kept in the font as a way for people to be reminded of their baptisms, it should be refreshed regularly; it is one thing to be "living water," it is another to have things living in the water!

The *Table*, or altar, as a liturgical center is the focal point for the celebration of the Eucharist, the sacrament commemorating Christ's Last Supper, the sacrifice on the Cross, and the Resurrection. The main feature of the sanctuary, it is often also the focal point of sacred architectural design—and a space where even in congregations with low Eucharistic piety, lay people rarely enter.

For our purposes, the altar has its origins in both Jewish sacrificial altars and the table around which the disciples sat for the Passover Meal, or the Last Supper. In other words, it signifies Christ's presence in the Eucharistic elements and the communal aspect of the sacrament as the congregation gathers to receive the Body and Blood of Christ in Holy Communion.

When it comes to adornment of the altar, the Book of Common Prayer only requires that "the Holy Table is spread with a clean white cloth during the celebration." [406] The use of candles, a cross, and other antependia vary based on tradition and custom of each congregation. We will spend more time on this in our upcoming discussion of the Holy Eucharist.

A possible final liturgical center to consider is the *presider's chair*. Through the 4th century, much of the liturgy was led, and the sermon even preached, from the presider's chair. Today, our seating is as varied as our architecture. If presidency of the liturgy occurs from seats, they need to be distinct and visible to the congregation and, while mainly a convenience, the chair "ought to be designed and located with reticence and not resemble a throne."[4]

What we have discussed above are the main liturgical spaces and centers. There are many other terms often associated with the architectural and liturgical aspects of churches. Let's delve into a few common ones here.

The *sanctuary* is the immediate area around the altar where the liturgical rites are performed, usually separated by the altar rail where Communion is often administered. The term itself originates from the Latin "*sanctuarium*," which means a place for sacred things. It can also refer more broadly to the entire chancel area or even the entire worship space. Of interesting note, it was also a place of refuge where fugitives could seek protection by the Church; in contemporary times, some congregations have protected those they believe are being unjustly targeted by the government (i.e. refugees, immigrants, certain protestors).

In some architecture, the sanctuary is housed in an *apse*, which is a semicircular or polygonal recess of a church. The term comes from the Latin *apsis*, meaning "arch" or "vault." Apse construction dates to Roman architecture and early Christian basilicas and is designed to provide a focal point for the altar.

In medieval and renaissance architecture, a backdrop for the altar was provided and is called a *reredos*. This ornamental screen or wall behind the altar is often decorated with carvings, statues,

---

4. Ibid, 89

and paintings, enhancing its visual importance and focus. The word reredos comes from the Old French *areredos* (which is a combination of *arere* meaning "behind" and *dos* meaning "back").

The word *chancel* derives from the Latin word *cancelli* which is translated as "lattice." Originally, this referred to the area beyond the screen or latticework that separated the choir seating from the nave. Over time, the term came to denote the entire area beyond this screen including the choir and clergy seating and the altar.

The *Quire* (often spelled *Choir* in the United States) is the area of the church where, logically, the choir sits, often situated between the nave and the sanctuary. Quire comes from the Latin *chorus*, meaning "a band of singers." In medieval monastic churches and cathedrals, the choir area became a very distinct architectural feature, often separated by screens and marked by stalls and other special seating.

A *rood screen* is a partition, often richly decorated, that separates the nave from the quire and chancel in a church. The word rood comes from the Old English word for "cross." These screens were common in medieval churches and often featured a crucifix and figures of Mary, the Mother of Jesus, and John, the beloved disciple. They served to visually and symbolically separate the clergy from the laity.

The *nave* is the central part of a church, extending from the entrance (the narthex) to the chancel, and is typically flanked by aisles. The word comes from the Latin word for ship, *navis*, because of the ship-like appearance of the vaulted ceiling. It is the main body of the church where the congregation sits.

Some of our congregations will also have a *chapel*, which is a smaller place of worship and it has a fascinating historical context. Chapel comes from the Latin *capella*, which means "a little cloak." It is linked to St. Martin of Tours, a 4th century Roman soldier who became a bishop. He is renowned for his act of charity of cutting his military cloak in half to share with a beggar during a snowstorm. The half of the cloak he retained became a revered relic, preserved in a special shrine by the Frankish kings. The shrine was called the *capella* and the custodians of the relic were known as *cappellani* (chaplains).

As Christianity spread, the term chapel evolved to describe various small worship spaces both in larger churches for devotionals, memorials, smaller liturgies or guild worship and within castles, manor houses, and other private estates for household use. Today, chapels can be found in diverse settings, including hospitals, schools, military bases, airports, and universities, serving as places for prayer, reflection, and worship.

A *chantry* is a particular type of chapel. It is dedicated to the memory of the founder or others specified by the donor. The term derives from the Anglo-French word *chanterie* from *chanter* meaning "to sing." Chantries became popular in the Middle Ages as a means for wealthy patrons to ensure prayers were said for their souls after death.

These terms reflect the rich architectural and liturgical traditions of Christian churches, evolving over centuries to meet both functional and symbolic needs within the context of worship and religious practice. There is much more that could be considered with regard to our church buildings and worship spaces: stained glass, ceramics, painting, mosaics, sculpture, book-binding, icons, graphic arts, posters, banners, needle-point, electronic media, and more.

One can see why it might be easy to end up with "*Aida* in a phone booth" in our church buildings. Good leaders of liturgy should keep in mind the goal of all our liturgical space, and its accompanying adornments, is to enable worshippers to encounter a deeper understanding of and greater connection to Christ.

Jesus entered our world in a time and place. Throughout Scripture, we learn of God's saving actions among humanity where they dwelt— not in some distant or remote place to which they needed to venture, but in ordinary places. Also, we know those ordinary places were marked as holy or sacred by those people and the generations that followed.

Congregations were established in places where our ancestors encountered God's work in their midst and these places were then marked as sacred. Today, as custodians of the sacred, the Altar Guild should consider the incarnational reality of God at work in this time and place and help create liturgical spaces and centers that enhance worship, support the liturgy's movement, and foster a sense of sacredness and community.

Almighty God, to whose glory the Altar Guild ministers in your house of prayer: thanks and praise are yours for the fellowship of those who have worshiped here, and prayer offered that all who seek you here may find you, and be filled with your joy and peace; through Jesus Christ our Lord, who lives and reigns with you, in the unity of the Holy Spirit, one God, now and for ever. Amen. [254, adapted]

CHAPTER FIVE

THE BOOK
OF COMMON PRAYER

There was never any thing by the wit of man so well devised, or so sure established, which in continuance of time hath not been corrupted: as, among other things, it may plainly appear by the common prayers in the Church, commonly called Divine Service...

From the Preface to the first Book of Common Prayer[1]

We know that communal worship occurs in a specific time and place. Our last chapter centered on the place, discussing the liturgical spaces and centers of our church buildings; and our attention will turn to time in our next chapter. Here our focus is on the foundation for how Episcopalians "do" liturgy.

The idea of *order* has been an important part of liturgy from the earliest days. In writing to the Corinthians, St. Paul reminded worship leaders that "all things should be done decently and in order" (1 Cor 14:40). The English word "order" comes from the Latin word *ordo,* which means to arrange things in a structured manner. In a subsequent chapter on the Holy Eucharist, we will discuss a deeper, more profound theological meaning of *ordo,* creating for us a distinction between ordo and order. In this chapter, our attention is on the development of the prescribed way in which we conduct liturgy with its sequence of prayers, readings, hymns, and rituals.

---

1. *The First and Second Prayer Book of Edward VI* (New York: Dutton, 1952), 3. Spelling modernized.

Our guide for creating that order in worship is the Book of Common Prayer. Jeffrey Lee, the now-retired Bishop of Chicago, in his work *Opening the Prayer Book*, noted:

> The words and forms of *The* Book of Common Prayer define our corporate identity perhaps to a degree not true of any other churches—even those with strong liturgical traditions. And not only are the words important for us, the book itself has a tremendous influence on our sense of who we are.[2]

The Book of Common Prayer is a foundational text for worship in Anglicanism, shaping practice and theological understanding for centuries. Its development reflects the evolution of Anglicanism itself, as well as broader shifts in religious, social, and even political landscapes. For Episcopalians, the 1979 edition of the Book of Common Prayer stands as the culmination of this historical trajectory. In it, and the subsequently approved liturgical resources, our worship finds an integration of diverse theological perspectives and contemporary concerns. To understand its significance, we must trace its development from its earliest iterations.

King Henry VIII of England reigned from 1509 to 1547. Frustrated by Pope Clement VII's refusal to annul his marriage to Catherine of Aragon because of political concerns, Henry separated himself from the authority of the Pope and was established as Supreme Governor over the Church in England through the Act of Supremacy in 1534. Not only did this action allow the annulment of his marriage (and permit his subsequent remarriages), but Henry's actions also led to significant religious and political changes. At first, liturgy in parishes did not change significantly; Henry considered himself a Catholic, even if not in union with the Pope. Things changed upon Henry's death, and over the next

---

2. Lee, Jefferey. *Opening the Prayer Book*. The New Church's Teaching Series: Volume Seven. (Cambridge: Cowley Publications, 1999), 5.

century, for better or worse, the practice of faith was tied closely to the English monarch.

The 1549 Book of Common Prayer, compiled primarily by Archbishop of Canterbury Thomas Cranmer under the reign of Henry's son, Edward VI, marks the beginning of the English Reformation's significant influence on liturgical practice. This new universal prayer book consolidated various forms of worship and multiple liturgical books into a single volume, providing a standardized framework for communal worship in the Church of England. Primarily, it represented a significant departure from the Latin Mass since by Cranmer's design "all things shall be read and sung in the church in the English tongue, to the end that the congregation may be thereby edified."[3] Drawing, however, from medieval liturgical traditions, particularly those of Hereford, Lincoln, and Salisbury, as well as continental Reformation influences, the prayer book made a start at the English Reformation's significant impact on liturgical practice and proved to be a balance of Catholic tradition and Protestantism.

Within just few years, the on-going religious reformation in England sought to align the liturgy of the Church of the England even more with Reformed theology. The 1552 Book of Common Prayer, also compiled under Edward VI and Archbishop Cranmer, further distanced the Church from Roman Catholic traditions.

For example, the so-called "Black Rubric" was added that explicitly stated that kneeling during the celebration of Holy Communion was intended purely as a gesture of reverence and humility before God, not as an act of worship directed at the consecrated elements themselves. Several other traditional elements, such as the use of vestments and certain ceremonies, were also minimized or removed. This prayer book was part of the broader movement to establish

---

3. "The Preface," *The First and Second Prayer Book of Edward VI* (New York: Dutton, 1952), 5. Spelling modernized.

a distinctly Protestant identity within the Church of England. Its adoption faced great resistance, leading to its temporary suspension under Queen Mary I, who restored Catholic practices from 1553 until her death in 1558, when Queen Elizabeth I restored the Protestant faith to England.

With a new monarch came a new prayer book. The 1559 Book of Common Prayer was a pivotal revision aimed at consolidating the English Reformation. Following the tumultuous reigns of Edward VI and Mary I, this edition sought to establish religious stability and a moderate Protestant settlement. The 1559 edition largely followed the 1552 edition but included some conciliatory changes to appease both traditionalists and reformers. Notably, it reinstated the use of some liturgical vestments and altered the wording of the Communion service to include elements from the 1549 prayer book, which had been more acceptable to conservative factions. This prayer book also played a crucial role in shaping Anglican liturgy and doctrine and laying the foundation for the Elizabethan Religious Settlement, which brought an end to the English Reformation period. However, it did not end theological and liturgical disagreements between Catholics and Protestants, which may have been as much political as it was religious.

The 1604 Book of Common Prayer emerged during the reign of King James I. This edition was primarily a response to the Hampton Court Conference, where the King met with Anglican bishops and Puritan leaders to address grievances and potential reforms in the Church of England. It was also from this conference that work began on the King James Bible (1611).

The 1662 Book of Common Prayer must be understood in its unique historical context. The English Civil War began in 1639 and culminated in the execution of King Charles I in 1649 and the establishment of the Commonwealth. During the Interregnum Period from 1649 to 1660, the use of the Book of Common Prayer was prohibited, and Puritan forms of worship were imposed. The monarchy was restored in 1660 and King Charles II took to the English throne. During the Restoration, there was a concerted effort to reinstate traditional Anglican worship while addressing some of the Puritans' concerns.

This process was overseen by a group of bishops and theologians who aimed to produce a text that balanced Catholic and Anglican tradition, Puritanism, and on-going theological development. Parliament approved this new Book of Common Prayer in 1662.

Though additional resources are added with more regularity than in the Episcopal Church, the 1662 edition remains the official prayer book of the Church of England. To this day, it remains one of the most enduring editions in Anglicanism with its influence extended to the churches of the Anglican Communion.

A Prayer Book for America

When, in the course of Divine Providence, these American States became independent with respect to civil government, their Ecclesiastical Independence was necessarily included; and the different religious denominations of Christians in these States were left at full and equal liberty to model and organize their respective churches and forms of worship, and discipline, in such manner as they might judge most convenient for their future prosperity.[4]

—From the Preface to the Book of Common Prayer (1789)

Published in 1789, the newly-formed Episcopal Church's Book of Common Prayer was shaped by the unique context of the post-Revolutionary United States of America. Prior to the American Revolution, the Church of England had been the established Church in many colonies, with Anglican liturgy and governance shaping religious practice. However, the break with Britain necessitated the

---

4. Book of Common Prayer (Philadelphia: Young and Ormond, 1795) via Google Books, digitized 2017. Language modernized.

reorganization of religious institutions and the establishment of new ecclesiastical structures separate from political authorities.

In the years immediately following the Revolution, Episcopal congregations in America faced the challenge of adapting Anglican liturgy to their new political and ecclesiastical circumstances. Some continued to use the 1662 Book of Common Prayer, while others sought to develop their own forms of worship. These early attempts at liturgical adaptation reflected the diversity of theological perspectives and regional differences within the Episcopal Church.

Understandably, this lack of a standardized liturgy posed challenges for the unity and coherence of the Episcopal Church in America. Recognizing the need for a common prayer book that would provide stability, the newly formed General Convention of the Episcopal Church convened in 1785 to address this issue. The convention appointed a committee to prepare a prayer book specifically tailored to meet the needs of American congregations.

Drawing upon the English Book of Common Prayer (1662), as well as liturgical texts from the Episcopal Church of Scotland—by whom our first bishop, Samuel Seabury, was ordained—the committee worked diligently to create a prayer book that would reflect the unique identity and aspirations of this new Church in the Anglican tradition. The 1789 American Book of Common Prayer retained much of the structure and content of the 1662 English Book of Common Prayer while incorporating modifications to reflect the American political and ecclesiastical independence and diverse religious context.

Primary among these differences are the prayers for civil authorities. Gone were the prayers for the King; these new prayers were tailored to the American political context, emphasizing the principles of republican government and the welfare of the newfound nation. These prayers affirmed the Church's on-going commitment to civic engagement and social responsibility.

Second, and of great importance, was the structure for the liturgy of the Eucharist. While generally it retained the basic structure of the familiar English prayer book, it incorporated the inclusion of the *epiclesis*, or invocation of the Holy Spirit, in the prayer of consecration from the Scottish rite. This shifted the theological understanding of the Lord's Supper from the Puritan simple memorial to one that reflects the real presence of Christ in Holy Communion.

Over the next century, minor revisions were made to the prayer book and additions of hymns, metrical psalms, occasional prayers and the like were added to what became known as the Prayer Book Collection. By the mid-1800s, profound transformation was taking place American religious and societal life. Industrialization, urbanization, and immigration from across Europe and beyond—plus our own Civil War—led to social upheaval and cultural change. It became clear the church needed new liturgical resources to speak to these societal changes.

William Reed Huntington, a prominent figure in the Episcopal Church in the 19th century, began calling for the full revision of the prayer book. A committee of General Convention was finally formed in 1871 to review proposals for liturgical enrichment and flexibility of use, especially in growing and diverse urban centers. After two decades of discussion, only minor revisions were made in 1892.

The early decades of the 20th century were marked by social, cultural, and technological upheaval. Simultaneously, the Episcopal Church, like other denominations, grappled with the challenges and opportunities presented by modernity, World War I, and renewed interest in biblical theology, liturgical renewal, early Church writings, and ecumenism.

By 1913, it was apparent that the revisions of 1892 were inadequate and further revision would be necessary. A resolution was passed calling for the appointment of a committee to undertake a comprehensive revision of the prayer book. Again, only minor revisions, targeted at increased enrichment and flexibility, were made in 1928. However, a key decision was made at the General Convention of 1928: the establishment of the Standing Liturgical Commission (today called the Standing Commission on Liturgy and Music). Its primary role was to prepare for the full revision of the Book of Common Prayer.

The liturgical renewal movement, begun in the late 1800s in the Oxford Movement in England, had taken hold across the Western world by the 1930s. The impetus for this revision gained momentum at the 1964 General Convention when a resolution was passed calling for concrete proposals for full revision of the prayer book by the Standing Liturgical Commission.

Over the next decade, the Commission offered proposals for the celebration of the Holy Eucharist and other services and the General Convention approved them for trial use. Many still remember the different colored paperback books that appeared in our pews. Feedback was gathered from across dioceses, parishes, and select committees—as broad a cross-section of laity and clergy as possible. Finally, a proposed Book of Common Prayer was published in 1976, which was used widely across the Church. In 1979, both houses of General Convention approved its use as the official Book of Common Prayer.

While a significant revision, this prayer book still reflects the values of the first Book of Common Prayer in 1549: "fidelity to the Scriptures and the liturgy of the early Church, the unifying of the realm (i.e. the Church) and the edification of the people."[5] Similarly, much of the 1928 prayer book, and thus the first American prayer book (1789), was retained in some form. However, the early Church practice of centrality of the Eucharist in worship is restored and it introduced a more flexible liturgical structure, offering multiple options for prayers and services to accommodate various congregational needs. The language was updated to be more expansive and contemporary, while retaining traditional elements. Updated prayers and new rites for baptism, marriage, and burial were also included, reflecting broader

5. Hatchett, Marion. *Commentary on the American Prayer Book.* (New York: Harpers Collins, 1995), 13.

and ecumenical liturgical renewal. Lay participation in the liturgy was also now emphasized.

The work for revision did not stop. The Standing Commission on Liturgy and Music continued the work begun in the early 1800s to continually provide new resources to add to the Prayer Book Collection, including new hymnals, multiple liturgical volumes, and revised church calendars.

The *Book of Occasional Services* is a supplemental resource providing liturgical resources for special occasions and events not covered in the Book of Common Prayer. The latest edition (2022) includes seasonal blessings; a variety of special liturgies, including Festivals of Lessons and Carols, a service for Our Lady of Guadalupe, Tenebrae, St. Francis Day and Blessing of the Animals and more; pastoral liturgies for welcoming people to the congregation, renaming, the catechumenate, healing, blessing of homes, and honoring God in creation; congregational liturgies for the founding or planting of a church or mission, the secularization of a church building, and distribution of Holy Communion by Lay Eucharistic Visitors; and, finally, episcopal services for the blessing of holy oils, the reaffirmation of ordination vows, the reception of clergy from other denominations, and the leave-taking from a congregation. The *Book of Occasional Services* is under constant review, evaluation, and revision.

Lesser Feasts and Fasts, first published in 1963 and revised many times since, supplements the Book of Common Prayer by offering optional commemorations for saints from various traditions and periods and notable figures throughout Church history. It provides readings, prayers, and biographical notes for those days. Most recently updated in 2022, this volume emphasizes the diverse and ongoing witness of the Christian faith and the evolving understanding and appreciation of sainthood within the Episcopal Church. Similar resources have included *Holy Women, Holy Men* and *Great Cloud of Witnesses*.

Enriching Our Worship is a series of supplemental liturgical resources developed by the Episcopal Church to enhance and expand the worship options available to congregations. The project began in the late 1990s in response to requests for additional liturgical materials that would reflect the diversity of the Church's worshiping communities and address emerging theological and cultural concerns. It reflects the Episcopal Church's commitment to inclusive and expansive worship, providing congregations with tools to engage more deeply with the liturgical life of the Church and to adapt worship to their specific contexts and needs. The series includes expanding resources for praying the Daily Office and the celebration of the Holy Eucharist, rites for healing and reconciliation, and prayers for various life events such as marriage, childbirth, and death. These resources draw upon the rich tradition of Anglican liturgy while incorporating elements from other Christian traditions as well as contemporary theological insights.

In 2018, the General Convention of the Episcopal Church considered a resolution calling again for the comprehensive revision of the Book of Common Prayer. The resolution sparked intense debate, with proponents arguing for the need to update the prayer book to better reflect contemporary theological understandings and cultural realities, and opponents expressing concerns about the potential disruption and division that could result from such a revision.

At the time of this publication, the General Convention has not yet decided to undertake a comprehensive revision of the Book of Common Prayer, opting instead to authorize the development of alternative liturgical texts and resources for experimental and possibly approved use. As the Episcopal Church continues to navigate the complexities of evolving theology, contemporary society, and remaining faithful to its heritage, this decision reflects the age-old Anglican practice of holding in tension tradition and innovation, continuity and change, for the sake of unity.

Almighty and everliving God, who through the Book of Common Prayer restored the language of the people in the prayers of your church: Make us always thankful for this heritage; and help us so to pray in the Spirit and with understanding, that we may worthily magnify your holy Name; through Jesus Christ our Lord, who lives and reigns with you and the Holy Spirit, one God, for ever and ever. Amen. [LFF, 253]

CHAPTER SIX

THE CHURCH YEAR

---

*So teach us to number our days ***
that we may apply our hearts to wisdom.

Psalm 90:12

"That's Super Bowl Sunday," a concerned voice said at a parish planning session. Planning for the next program year in our parishes and congregations usually begins with getting dates on the calendar—major feasts, federal holidays, school breaks, important regional events, and, of course, in my parish, the schedule for the Buffalo Bills.

Calendars are on our walls and desks and those on our computers, phones, and smart-watches ping and beep to alert us regularly. They give structure to, and often govern, all our lives and there are plenty of them to keep track of. In the Church, there is the fiscal year, the program year, and the Church year. While all these calendars influence the work of the Altar Guild in some way, our focus now turns specifically to the Church year—in general and then in more detail.

Massey H. Shepherd, Jr. was a prominent theologian and Episcopal priest who taught at the Episcopal Theological School in Cambridge, Massachusetts, and the Church Divinity School of the Pacific in Berkeley, California. He is best known for his contributions to liturgical scholarship and for his role in the 1979 revision of the Book of Common Prayer. Of the importance of the calendar, he wrote:

> The Christian year is a mystery through which every moment
> and all the times and seasons of this life are transcended and
> fulfilled in that reality which is beyond time. Each single holy

day, each single gospel pericope in the sequence of the year, is of itself a sacrament of the whole gospel. Each single feast renews the fullness and fulfillment of the Feast of feasts, our death and resurrection with Christ.[1]

For Shepherd, there is a connection between what is being celebrated and the reality of God's grace at work now and throughout salvation history. He argues that a sacramental quality exists as we think about what and how we celebrate points beyond itself to God at work. Thus, the Calendar provides more than a structured framework for communal worship: it offers us the opportunity for a cycle of theological reflection, spiritual discipline, and the formation of a shared Christian identity. Through the cyclical observance of liturgical seasons, Episcopalians engage in a dynamic and enriching journey of faith where we believe that God is still at work today as we remember past events in salvation history. Year after year, we tell the stories of the Kingdom of God to remind ourselves of how the Church is to look in the fullness of God's time. The Church Calendar isour guide leading us on this dynamic journey of faith.

The Two Cycles

To understand the role of the calendar as guide, it would be helpful to look at the year from the 30,000-foot view. The Book of Common Prayer notes: "The Church Year consists of two cycles of feasts and holy days: one is dependent upon the movable date of the Sunday of the Resurrection or Easter Day; the other, upon the fixed date of December 25, the Feast of our Lord's Nativity or Christmas Day." [15]

The paschal cycle relates to Easter, which as the high point of our Church year is when we celebrate the resurrection of Jesus, the Feast of feasts. It is the oldest festival of the Christian year. The

---

1. Shepherd, Massey. *Liturgy and Education* (New York: Seabury Press, 1955), 99.

paschal cycle begins on Ash Wednesday and concludes on the Day of Pentecost. Ash Wednesday begins Lent, the season of Lent, 40 day season of repentance and preparation for Easter. Holy Week begins with Palm Sunday and concludes with the Great Vigil of Easter. The Easter season itself begins with the Great Vigil of Easter and concludes on Pentecost.

The incarnational cycle centers on Christmas. It begins with the season of Advent and includes Epiphany and the subsequent celebration of the Baptism of Jesus. Advent is the four Sunday season prior to Christmas Day, which itself begins the twelve-day festival that concludes on the Feast of the Epiphany on January 6. Epiphany is then followed immediately by the Baptism of Jesus on the Sunday following. This time on the Church calendar is more than the celebrating the birthday of Jesus; it is recognizing, and celebrating our participation in salvation seen through the lens of Christ's Incarnation.

The paschal and incarnational cycles are connected by the Sundays after the Epiphany and the Sundays after the Pentecost. The former connect our celebration of the incarnation to the resurrection whereas the latter teach us how to live into the reign of the Risen Christ now and connect us to the return, or final advent, of Christ which we celebrate on the first Sunday of Advent. Then, the cycles begin again, guiding our lives in liturgical communities as we deepen our faith and become more fully who God calls us to be.

Sundays

We are most acutely aware of these cycles Sunday-by-Sunday. Sunday serves as the cornerstone of Christian worship and spiritual practice. The resurrection, which Scripture teaches us occurred on the first day of the week, transformed Sunday into the Lord's Day, a day for rejoicing and celebration. Sunday is also the first day of creation and the day when the Holy Spirit was sent to be our advocate and guide.

The hymn "O Day of Radiant Gladness" speaks meaningfully to the Scriptural and liturgical understanding of Sundays:

1 O day of radiant gladness,
  O day of joy and light,
  O balm of care and sadness,
  most beautiful, most bright;
  this day the high and lowly,
  through ages joined in tune,
  sing, "Holy, holy, holy,"
  to the great God Triune.

2 This day at the creation,
  the light first had its birth;
  this day for our salvation
  Christ rose from depths of earth;
  this day our Lord victorious
  the Spirit sent from heaven,
  and thus this day most glorious
  a triple light was given.[2]

This well-known hymn has its roots in the earliest Christian practices. From the beginnings of the Church down through the centuries to this very day, our gatherings are held not just out of practicality but with deep symbolism in mind. Justin Marytr, a 2nd century Christian apologist and philosopher, wrote: "We all hold this common gathering on Sunday since it is the *first day*, on which God transforming darkness and matter made the universe, and Jesus Christ our Savior rose from the dead on the same day."[3] We know that

---

2. Wordsworth, Christopher. "O Day of Radiant Gladness." The Hymnal 1982. (New York: Church Hymnal Corporation, 1985), 48.

3. Justin Martyr, *I Apology 67* in Johnson, Maxwell. *Sacraments and Worship: The Sources of Christian Theology*. Westminster John Knox, 2012. (Emphasis is mine)

the first followers of Jesus gathered on Sundays, apart from regular Jewish sabbath observances, to offer prayers, tell the stories of Jesus, and share in a communal meal. Quickly the Sunday observance took hold forboth Gentiles and Jews as the message of Jesus spread, and the gathering of the nascent Christian community grew to include a sacramental life that reinforced their faith and mission in the world.

It should be noted here that we would do well to avoid the temptation to call the Lord's Day the sabbath or the "Christian sabbath," as some have over the centuries. It is a misappropriation of the word sabbath for what we do on Sundays or, worse in this author's opinion, for a day off from work. The Lord's Day is a unique Christian feast. The Episcopal Church recognizes the importance of rest and recreation, in line with the biblical Sabbath principle and it encourages a balance between worship, work, and rest for all people. Following the ancient custom of the Jewish faith, sabbath remains the last day of the week, our Saturday; it is a holy day of rest, as we are told in Genesis that on the seventh day God rested and sanctified a day of rest. Our prayer book acknowledges this in our collect for Saturday in the office of Morning Prayer recalling that God "sanctified a day of rest for all [God's] creatures," in order that we "may be duly prepared for the service of [the] sanctuary." [99]

Our tradition and practices hold that Sunday is not merely one feast among many: it is the "principal feast," as the prayer book explicitly states. This distinction elevates Sunday above other holy days and underscores its role as a weekly mini-Easter. As the weekly commemoration of the resurrection of Jesus Christ, it shapes the worship, prayer life, and communal identity of the Church. Our prayer book provides collects (or prayers) for each Sunday reflecting the themes of the Church season, as well as a comprehensive and diverse three-year lectionary that grounds our congregations in the biblical narrative and the story of salvation.

The ancient and fundamental act of worship on Sunday is the Holy Eucharist. The *Didache*, also known as "The Teaching of the

Twelve Apostles," is one of the earliest Christian documents outside the New Testament. Dating from the late first or early 2nd century, it offers instructions on Christian ethics, rituals, practices, and church organization. In the *Didache,* Christians are instructed "to assemble on the Lord's Day, and break bread and give thanks."[4] This was the pattern for centuries until the late Medieval period when the superabundance of saint days and other commemorations and feasts muddied the calendar and Sunday all but lost its prominence.

Following the reformations of the 16th and 17th centuries, in Anglicanism the Eucharist was celebrated far less frequently in most parishes, with Morning Prayer functioning as the primary Sunday liturgy. In many parishes, this continued until the 1979 revision of the Book of Common Prayer which restored the practice of weekly Sunday Eucharist, officially recognizing the trend that began in the liturgical renewal movement of the mid-to-late 19th century(More on this in the upcoming chapter on the Eucharist). While generally an anomaly today, some parishes still retain the practice of Morning Prayer some or most Sundays as the primary means of worship by their community. Whatever the practice of your congregation, the function of the Lord's Day remains the same: it is the primary day on the which your community of Christians gathers and from which the remainder of the week extends.

Holy Days and other Feasts and Fasts

Throughout the year, the calendar is punctuated by principal feasts, holy days, major feasts, fasts, lesser feasts, and days of optional devotion. These days are extensions of our Sunday liturgy and have liturgical, spiritual, and formational components.

In addition to those mentioned already, principal feasts include Ascension Day, Trinity Sunday, and All Saints' Day (November 1 and/or the Sunday following). These feasts always take precedence

---

4. See Johnson, Maxwell. *Sacraments and Worship: The Sources of Christian Theology.* Westminster John Knox, 2012.

on the calendar. Certain holy days take precedence over the Sunday calendar and these include: Holy Name (January 1), when we remember Jesus' naming and circumcision according to Jewish law; the Presentation (February 2), when we remember Jesus' presentation and dedication in the Temple; and, the Transfiguration (August 6), when we remember Moses and Elijah appearing with a transfigured Jesus to the disciples. Other Feasts of Our Lord, which do not take precedence over a Sunday, include: the Annunciation (March 25), the Visitation (May 31), St. John the Baptist (June 24), and Holy Cross Day (September 14). Other major feasts include those of apostles, evangelists, St. Mary the Virgin, St. Mary Magdalene, St. Michael and All Angels, as well as Independence Day and Thanksgiving Day.

The prayer book also provides for days of fasting and special devotion. Ash Wednesday and Good Friday are considered days of fasting; though, while customs exist, no provision for how to fast is given. Days marked by special devotion and discipline are:

> Ash Wednesday and the other weekdays of Lent and of Holy Week, except the feast of the Annunciation. Good Friday and all other Fridays of the year, in commemoration of the Lord's crucifixion, except for Fridays in the Christmas and Easter seasons, and any Feasts of our Lord which occur on a Friday. [17]

The Church has also given us lists of optional commemorations. The Reverend Ruth Meyers, Professor of Liturgy at the Church Divinity School of the Pacific, notes that calendars, such as *Lesser Feasts and Fasts*, "[help] us realize the depth and breadth of the communion of saints and to make some of its members real to us," and how we are called to live our lives of faith.[5] The prayer book does not require celebration or commemoration and some days will have little significance in one

---

5. Meyers, Ruth and Mitchell, Leonel. *Praying Shapes Believing: A Theological Commentary on the Book of Common Prayer*. (New York: Seabury, 2016), 33.

congregation and be a day of great celebration in another. In the end, however, all our celebrations and commemorations help us recognize, in one way or another, our partaking in God's salvific action in the world and our connection to each other and the communion of saints.

The Secular Calendar

Thomas Talley was an Episcopal priest and preeminent scholar of the 20th century, having served as Professor of Liturgics at the General Theological Seminary in New York City from 1971 until his retirement in 1990. Talley taught that liturgy is a social occasion and involves the details of time and season.[6] Today, for us, part of the details of time and season is knowing that cultural and secular calendars also play a major role in our congregations. Whether it is Mother's Day, a harvest festival, the annual blessing of the fleet, or the like, these days, festivals, or events are important parts of the lives of our communities and should be regarded as such. While incorporating them should be done carefully and thoughtfully, their remembrance in our liturgies helps to connect our faith to the world in which *we live and move and have our being*.

In the end, the diversity of festivals—sacred and secular—guide our year and the liturgies that we keep. They speak to us of our union in Christ's fellowship and prayer within the mystical body of Christ and, with sacramental quality, point us beyond ourselves to God at work in the Church and in the world from the beginning of creation to this very day.

> Heavenly Father, in you we live and move and have our being: We humbly pray you so to guide and govern us by your Holy Spirit, that in all the cares and occupations of our life we may not forget you, but may remember that we are ever walking in your sight; through Jesus Christ our Lord. Amen. [100]

---

6. See Vogel, Dwight, ed. *Primary Sources of Liturgical Theology: A Reader.* (Collegeville: The Liturgical Press, A Pueblo Book, 2000), 91.

CHAPTER SEVEN

SEASONS AND HOLY DAYS

"For everything there is a season, and a time for every matter under heaven."

Ecclesiastes 3:1

Camelot is the 1960 musical produced by Frederick Loewe and Alan Jay Lerner. Adapted from the 1958 novel *The Once and Future King* by T. H. White, it is based on the legend of King Arthur. In the last act of the musical, King Arthur commissions a young knight named Tom, saying:

Each evening from December to December,
before you drift to sleep upon your cot,
think back upon all the tales you remember-of Camelot.
Ask every person if he's heard the story—
and tell it strong and clear if he has not—
that once there was a fleeting wisp of glory called Camelot.[1]

King Arthur wanted the story of the glory that was Camelot to live on. Christians share a similar calling as Sir Tom to proclaim a message of a kingdom—the Kingdom of God. As we learned in last chapter, the Church year provides us a foundation for the proclamation of God's reign of justice, mercy, truth, and love. Liturgical Christians could easily replace 'December to December' with 'from Advent to Advent'—and so that is where we begin.

---

1. Lerner, Alan Jay. "Camelot." *Camelot*, 1960.

Advent

The word Advent is derived from the Latin word *adventus* meaning "coming." Advent marks the beginning of the Church year, and it includes the four Sundays before Christmas. Advent observances began as early as the 4th century. It serves as both a time of preparation and anticipation for both Christ's eventual return and the celebration of the birth of Jesus Christ. The season is characterized by themes of hope, expectation, and penitence.

The First Sunday of Advent looks forward to the return of Christ at the end of time—this is the eschatological theme that underscores the season. Eschatology is a branch of theology concerned with the final events of history, the ultimate destiny of humanity, and the world. In Christian theology, it focuses on concepts such as the Second Coming of Christ, the resurrection of the dead, the Last Judgment, and the establishment of God's reign in its fullness.

The second and third Sundays focuses on John the Baptist, the forerunner of Christ. John the Baptist was born to Zechariah, a priest, and Elizabeth, who was related to Mary, the mother of Jesus. An angel announced John's birth to Zechariah while he was performing his priestly duties at the altar in the temple. John's ministry began in the wilderness of Judea, where he lived an ascetic life, clothed in camel's hair and sustained by a diet of locusts and wild honey. His primary message was one of repentance and preparation for the coming of the Kingdom of God. He called for people to turn away from their sins and be baptized as a sign of their repentance. We will hear of John's role in Jesus' baptism during Epiphany.

The fourth Sunday focuses on the events most immediately leading up to the birth of Jesus. In Year A, our attention is drawn to Joseph's vision: an angel appears to him to say that the child conceived by Mary is from the Holy Spirit and is to be named Jesus. In the other years, we focus on Mary in the stories of the Annunciation and the Visitation. Described in Luke 1:26-38, the Annunciation tells of the angel Gabriel's visit to Mary, a young woman in Nazareth. Gabriel announces that she will conceive a son by the Holy Spirit and Mary responds with faith and humility, saying, "Here am I, the servant of the Lord; let it be with me according to your word." (Luke 1:38) In Year B, we hear the story of the Visitation of Mary to her relative Elizabeth. Described in Luke 1:39-56, upon Mary's greeting, Elizabeth's baby—John the Baptist—leaps in her womb, and Elizabeth, filled with the Holy Spirit, proclaims Mary blessed among women and her child blessed. Mary responds with the *Magnificat*, a song praising God's greatness and mercy. (We will discuss this in the upcoming chapter on the Daily Office.)

Advent's role as we have seen is two-fold: to both prepare us for the return of Christ and to lead us to our celebration of Christmas. The message of this season is expressed not only in our Scripture but also in our liturgies and other symbols of the season.

The liturgical color for Advent was traditionally purple or violet. Increasingly many Episcopal churches have adopted blue for Advent. This practice is said to be rooted in the Sarum Rite, originating from Salisbury Cathedral in medieval England. Blue distinguishes the season from Lent and emphasizes hope and expectation. Some parishes may use rose or pink vestments on the Third Sunday of Advent, known as Gaudete Sunday. *Gaudete* is the Latin word for "rejoice" and is taken from the first word of the ancient introit sung on that Sunday. The use of rose or pink vestments symbolizes the joy that Christ has brought into the world. The use of pink vestments and hangings often coincides with the use of a pink candle in the Advent Wreath.

The Advent wreath, a circle of evergreen branches with four candles (and often a fifth larger candle in the center called the Christ Candle) is a prominent symbol during this season. Historically, it was a devotion limited to the home; however, over time it began to be used in the sanctuary. Each Sunday, a new candle is lit, representing progressively the light of Christ coming into the world. The attachment of meaning to each candle is a contemporary innovation. No ceremony is prescribed for the lighting of the candles; they are simply lit when other candles are lit. If colored candles are used, they should match the color of the vestments and altar hangings. Consideration should be given to the placement of the wreath; while its visibility is important, it should not interfere with the liturgical centers, which we discussed in an earlier chapter.

Many churches hold special services during Advent. The *Book of Occasional Services* provides an order for Advent Festival Lessons and Carols. This service is a blending of scriptural readings with corresponding hymns and anthems that help us look forward to our celebration of Christmas. Since the primary act of worship on the Lord's Day is the Eucharist, this service is usually held apart from Sunday morning.

There may be additional Advent services in your congregations. Some parishes will hold a "Longest Night" or "Blue Christmas" service for those who are in mourning or find Advent and Christmas a difficult time to celebrate. The recent revisions of the *Book of Occasional Services* provide liturgies for the Feast of Our Lady of Guadalupe—a recognition of the diversity in our Church. Some clergy may wish to hold special mid-week liturgies as part of special Advent spiritual and formational programming.

The list could be endless, but one thing is clear: Advent is a season rich with liturgical, scriptural, and devotional elements that invites believers to prepare their hearts and minds for the coming of Christ. It is a time of both solemn reflection and joyful anticipation, drawing us into a deeper understanding of the promise of Christ's return and the mystery of the Incarnation.

Christmas

Christmas is a twelve-day festival that begins on December 25th and ends on the Feast of the Epiphany (January 6). This season is a time of celebration and deep theological reflection when we are invited to enter into the mystery of the Incarnation. Through our liturgies, music, and traditions, we are drawn into a deeper understanding of God's redemptive work and the ongoing call to live out the implications of the Incarnation in our daily lives.

The central mystery and theological idea celebrated at Christmas is this: "And the Word became flesh and lived among us, and we have seen his glory, the glory as of a father's only son, full of grace and truth" (John 1:14). The doctrine of the Incarnation speaks to the core of Christian faith—that in Jesus Christ, God entered human history, taking on human flesh to redeem and restore creation. It also affirms the inherent goodness of all humanity and underscores the intimate relationship between humanity and God, "who wonderfully created, and yet more wonderfully restored, the dignity of human nature," as the Collect for the Second Sunday after Christmas Day notes. [214]

Christmas also invites reflection on themes of light and darkness, hope and fulfillment, and the transformative power of God's love. The Nativity story, with its humble beginnings in a manger, challenges believers to recognize God's presence in the ordinary and the overlooked, calling us to lives of compassion, service, and witness.

While Christmas Day is December 25, the season in practice begins on the evening (or increasingly during the afternoon) of December 24 with the celebration of Christmas Eve to mark the transition from Advent to Christmas. These services are characterized by the reading of the Nativity story, the singing of carols, and the celebration of the Holy Eucharist. The liturgical color changes to white or gold, symbolizing glory, joy, and light. (While the liturgical color of white was often said to be associated with "purity," we would do well to be mindful of how this idea has been used negatively to imply that *non-white* is somehow impure.)

Known also as Christmastide, the festive twelve days are a time of continued celebration and reflection on the mystery of the Incarnation. Each day within this period holds particular significance, and the prayer book provides specific collects and readings for use throughout Christmastide. Immediately following Christmas are the major feasts of St. Stephen, the first martyr of the Church (December 26) and St. John the Evangelist, who penned the great hymn to the incarnation found in the opening verses of John's Gospel (December 27). Holy Innocents (December 28) remembers the account of King Herod's tragic slaughter of children out of fear that Jesus would challenge his kingship, the on-going reality of suffering and violence, and our calling in Christ to work for justice and peace.

January 1 is the Feast of the Holy Name of Jesus. It is a feast celebrating the naming and circumcision of Jesus as described in Luke 2:21. This day underscores the importance of Jesus' name, which means "God saves," and reflects on Christ's identity and mission. The liturgical focus of this feast is prayers and hymns that honor the name of Jesus and its significance for Christians. Sometimes combined with a New Year's Eve/Day Service, this feast always takes precedence on Sundays.

During these twelve days, many Episcopal churches continue to hold special services and children's pageants. Some parishes offer a Festival of Lessons and Carols for Christmas, which combines scriptural readings with Christmas hymns, carols, and anthems to tell the story of salvation from the fall of Adam and Eve to the birth of Christ. This tradition reinforces the theological understanding of Christmas as part of the broader narrative of God's redemptive plan.

All of our liturgies and pageants point to the importance of in our lives today. As the philosopher-theologian Josef Pieper notes: "If the incarnation of God is no longer understood as an event that directly concerns the present lives of men [and women], it becomes impossible, even absurd, to celebrate Christmas festively."[2]

---

2. See Meyers, Ruth and Mitchell, Leonel. *Praying Shapes Believing: A Theological Commentary on the Book of Common Prayer*. (New York: Seabury, 2016), 14.

Feast of the Epiphany, Baptism of Our Lord, and the Season after Epiphany

The Christmas season ends on January 6th with the Feast of the Epiphany, which celebrates the revelation of Christ to the Gentiles as represented by the visit of the Magi (Wise Men) to the infant Jesus (Matthew 2:1-12). Epiphany, from the Greek word meaning "manifestation" or "appearance," highlights the theme of light and revelation, emphasizing that Jesus is the Savior of all people.

The liturgical color for the Feast of the Epiphany itself is white or gold, symbolizing joy, light, and celebration. In some places, the feast will include the blessing of chalk and the marking of doorways with the inscription of the Magi's initials and the year, a practice that invokes God's blessing on homes. [e.g., 20+C+M+B+25]

On the first Sunday after the Epiphany we remember the Baptism of Our Lord. On this day, we hear again the story of John baptizing Jesus in the Jordan River, which marks the beginning of Jesus' public ministry. During the baptism, as the heavens open, and the Holy Spirit descends on Jesus like a dove, a voice from heaven proclaimed, "This is my Son, the Beloved, with whom I am well pleased" (Matthew 3:17). As a forerunner of Christ, John also acknowledged his subordinate role to Jesus, stating, "He must increase, but I must decrease" (John 3:30). This is one of the days that the Book of Common Prayer designates as particularly appropriate for baptisms. Often if there are no baptisms, congregations will replace the Nicene Creed with the renewal of their Baptismal Covnenant.

In the weeks after Epiphany, key events in Jesus' ministry are remembered, such as: his first miracle of changing water into wine at a wedding in Cana; early accounts of his healings; the calling of the disciples; and important moments in his preaching. These events help to reveal Jesus as Divine and encourage us to explore more deeply our role as members of Christ's Body in revealing him to the world. This is expressed best in the seasonal blessing proposed for this season:

"may Christ the Son of God be manifest in you that your lives may be a light to the world." [BOS, 12]

Beginning with the Second Sunday after the Epiphany, the liturgical color of the season is green. Green is the color often associated with what is sometimes called "ordinary time:" the seasons between Pentecost and Advent and Epiphany and Lent. Green represents life and during Epiphany we speak of how we live as people of the Incarnation in the world.

The Feast of the Presentation (February 2nd) falls during the Season after the Epiphany. As we saw with Holy Name, this feast takes precedence over a Sunday. This feast commemorates Jesus' presentation to God in the Temple on the fortieth day after his birth in accordance with Jewish law. Continuing the theme of the season, this is a moment of manifestation of Jesus as the Messiah, when Old and New Testament come together in the encounter with the priest Simeon and the prophetess Anna. The prayer and words of Simeon are a part of our evening liturgies and we will discuss those in an upcoming chapter. Also, in keeping with the theme of the season, the Simeon calls Jesus a light to the world. For this reason, candles have historically been blessed during a liturgy on this day, giving the feast the name Candlemas (or Candle Mass). In Tudor England, this marked the end of the Christmas season—in other words, if you haven't taken your Christmas Tree down yet, this is the day!

The length of the season varies based on the date for Ash Wednesday. The season can be as short as four Sundays or as long as nine Sundays. The Sunday before Lent begins we always read the Gospel account of Jesus' transfiguration. This should not be called Transfiguration Sunday or the like, however; the Feast of the Transfiguration is properly celebrated on August 6. The Gospel lesson for the Last Sunday after the Epiphany is chosen primarily because it marks the turning point in the story of Jesus as he sets his eyes towards Jerusalem and his death and resurrection. The color of the day may switch to white or gold to signal this celebration. This

Sunday is the last time the word *Alleluia* is used until the Great Vigil of Easter. Your congregation may have some customs around "retiring the Alleluia" on this day. In the end, this Sunday points us to our Lenten pilgrimage toward the cross and Easter, which is about to begin.

Lent

During this season of pilgrimage, the nature of our liturgy will change: Music is often more reserved and as mentioned above, the word Alleluia is missing. Our prayers will reflect the penitential nature of the season. The decoration of the building and the use of vibrant color is often reduced; many congregations will suspend the use of flowers and other decorations. Purple or violet hangings and vestments are often used, though many use the old English custom of the Lenten Array, which are unbleached linen vestments with only simple symbols stenciled in black or oxblood red. If a congregation has rose or pink vestments, these would be used on the Fourth Sunday in Lent, as we note the joy of Easter approaching. In some congregations, crosses and statues are veiled with colored or unbleached fabric. Lent is a busy time for the Altar Guild and the checklists in the appendix reflect that.

The history and purpose season of Lent is best summed up by the Book of Common Prayer in the liturgy for Ash Wednesday:

> The first Christians observed with great devotion the days of our Lord's passion and resurrection, and it became the custom of the Church to prepare for them by a season of penitence and fasting. This season of Lent provided a time in which converts to the faith were prepared for Holy Baptism. It was also a time when those who, because of notorious sins, had been separated from the body of the faithful were reconciled by penitence and forgiveness, and restored to the fellowship of the Church. Thereby, the whole congregation was put in

mind of the message of pardon and absolution set forth in the Gospel of our Savior, and of the need which all Christians continually have to renew their repentance and faith. [264-5]

Calling the congregation into the commemoration of the season, the presider concludes, "I invite you, therefore, in the name of the Church, to the observance of a holy Lent, by self-examination and repentance; by prayer, fasting, and self-denial; and by reading and meditating on God's holy Word." [265]

First Day of Lent: Ash Wednesday

This invitation from the Church on this first day of Lent sets the pattern for our Lenten observance. It also leads to our recognition that we are, in fact, mortal and reliant on God's grace. The optional custom of the imposition ashes is to remind us of this mortality: "remember that you are dust and to dust you shall return," the presider says. [265] Ashes are not some sort of talisman or temporary tattoo of saintliness. Ashes are imposed in a gathering of Christians, who have acknowledged their sinfulness, and they are received in that context without pride or the perception of self-righteousness. (The question always remains, in light of the Gospel for the day where Jesus suggests we wash our faces when fasting [Matthew 6:1-6, 16-21], do we wash our ashes off before leaving?)

While the word "ash" may be in the title of the day, our attention in the liturgy focuses most on the invitation to a Holy Lent and the call of the Church to recognize our sinfulness and our need to repent and be changed by God's grace. Repentance is not the goal nor is it solely an individualistic act; repentance is about a renewed relationship with God, the community of the Church, and the world around us. We call this reconciliation.

As a result, the call to prayer, fasting, and self-denial are not merely about good works done for our own personal benefit (i.e. giving up desserts), but rather these disciplines free us, our time, and resources to better service and ministry. The Litany of Penitence [267] calls our attention to the ways in which we have strayed from God's commands, and we are put in mind of God's forgiveness and mercy and united with Christ and one another in the celebration of the Eucharist.

Popular modern culture has largely made Lent an individualistic endeavor, stripping it of its original meaning and the meaning deeply embedded in our liturgy. *Ashes to Go* has also become a fashionable custom in the last decade, almost to the point where in some congregations it is an assumed practice rather than an optional ritual act set within the context of a liturgical gathering of fellow believers. Altar Guild members might be called upon to assist. While it is hard to find the rationale for this practice within the theological underpinnings of the Book of Common Prayer, we have seen throughout history that approved liturgies occasionally follow years of common practice.

Sundays *in* Lent

The focus of our Lenten Sundays is to prepare us for Easter. It should be noted that these Sundays are said to be *in* Lent not *of* Lent and are thus not included in our counting of the 40 days of this season Sundays are always feast days and as this season is *lent* to us to prepare for Easter, we are people *in* preparation for Easter. In this preparation for Easter, rather than the focus being on the Gospel reading, we look to the Old Testament for the theme of the Sunday. There we are presented with a short course in the history of salvation: moments in the past when God's desire to save humanity is revealed. Each year, the readings from the Old Testament follow this pattern:

Lent 1: A story about the origins of humanity

Lent 2: A story about Abraham and Sarah

Lent 3: An account from the Exodus

Lent 4: An account of God restoring and reaffirming the covenant with God's people

Lent 5: A prophetic vision of the kingdom yet to come in its fullness.

As we gather on Sundays in Lent, we hear our story as people of God. Good liturgists and preachers will remind us that we still meet God today. Our individual and corporate devotional journeys through Lent join Christ's struggle and ultimate victory over evil and death celebrated on Easter.

Assist us mercifully with your help, O Lord God of our salvation, that we may enter with joy upon the contemplation of those mighty acts, whereby you have given us life and immortality; through Jesus Christ our Lord. Amen. [270]

Holy Week

Holy Week is our time for focused contemplation on the final days of Jesus' life. It begins on The Sunday of the Passion: Palm Sunday. Our liturgy that day begins with the Liturgy of the Palms, celebrating Jesus' entry into Jerusalem. In many congregations, a festive procession with palm branches takes place either within the church or moves there from another gathering point. Festive psalms and hymns, such as "All glory, laud, and honor," are sung. Again, liturgists, sacristans, and congregations would do well to remember that this isn't the focus of the day; the second part of the liturgy turns to the passion and death of Jesus, turning the day's attention to the crucifixion. As we move from triumph to tragedy, the account of the Lord's Passion is read from one of the synoptic Gospels—Matthew, Mark, or Luke.

The color of day, and most of Holy Week, is traditionally red. When it is used, the Altar Guild would do well to use a darker red, sometimes called Passiontide red or oxblood and avoid the vibrant and festive red of Pentecost. Violet or Lenten array may be used instead.

During the week, your congregation may hold daily Eucharists or other special services, such as Tenebrae, a medieval monastic office marked by the gradual extinguishing of candles. Like for church musicians, it is the busiest week for the Altar Guild with many extra liturgies and more work, most notably at the end of the week from Maundy Thursday through Easter Day, so plan wisely and focus your attention and energy carefully.

The Three Days

It has become increasingly common in the Episcopal Church to use the Latin word *Triduum* (meaning "three days") to refer to liturgies Maundy Thursday, Good Friday, and the Great Vigil of Easter. These liturgies are rooted in those of Jerusalem written about by Egeria, the late fourth century Roman Christian pilgrim who wrote extensively about her pilgrimage to the Holy Land. These days mark the end of the Lenten Season and the culmination of Holy Week, and are also the high-point of the Church year.

Maundy Thursday is our remembrance of the Last Supper and Jesus' institution of the sacrament of Holy Communion. The color of the day for hangings and vestments is often white, however some congregations will use Passiontide red or Lenten array , to distinguish from the white of Easter. The liturgy may include the foot-washing ceremony, when we recall Jesus washing of the disciples' feet as an act of extraordinary and unparalleled servitude and his declaration: "I give you a new commandment, that you love one another." (John 13:34) It is here we get the word Maundy: from the word *mandatum*, a Latin word meaning "commandment." As the disciples' festive Passover gathering celebrating Israel's delivery from slavery was overshadowed by Jesus' forthcoming betrayal and death, our celebration of the Eucharist this day is enveloped by the shadow of the cross.

Some parishes include an agape—or shared—meal before, during, or after the proper liturgy. It is hard to emphasize this enough: This is not a Christian seder; a seder is a sacred meal set in the context of a Jewish community during Passover. Provisions have been made in the *Book of Occasional Services* for orders for these meals. Thoughtful and creative liturgists and sacristans can find ways to connect an agape meal with the proper liturgy of the day.

The Maundy Thursday liturgy often concludes with the stripping of the altar: the removal of all vessels, paraments, crosses, candles, etc. from the chancel and sanctuary. No formal provisions are made by the Church and customs vary widely. The axiom "less is more" applies. Consideration should be given to when the action of stripping the altar becomes more chaos than a richly symbolic action in which the Altar Guild often plans a prominent role. Your ancestors the sacristans of the medieval church also used this as an opportunity to clean all the linens, vestments, vessels, and paraments—a tradition that often continues to this day behind the scenes. The congregation is invited to leave in silence and the sanctuary is left bare in preparation for the stark solemnity of the next day's liturgy.

Good Friday focuses on the crucifixion and death of Jesus. There is no celebration of the Eucharist on this day. Rooted in early liturgies of Jerusalem, Constantinople, Gaul, and Rome, the order for the day includes the reading from the Passion according to John[3], the Solemn Collects, anthems sung in honor of the cross, and the optional distribution of Holy Communion reserved the night before. The theme of the liturgy is best expressed in the collect, "Behold this your family, for whom our Lord Jesus Christ was willing to be betrayed." [276] The focus of the liturgy is the Solemn Collects when we kneel at the foot of the cross and plead for the needs of world to Christ, who is both crucified and risen—connecting the incarnational and paschal cycles discussed in the last chapter in one moment.

---

3. Wide consideration is being given to substituting or editing the Passion according to John because of the prolific use of the term "the Jews" and its historic justification for anti-semitism and the persecution of the Jewish people.

Other liturgies and devotionals, such as the Stations of the Cross, the daily offices or Tenebrae, may be offered on Good Friday. The color of the day is oxblood, violet, or black; the practice around the use of vestments varies widely.

Holy Saturday, or the holy sabbath, is marked by a very simple liturgy that references Jesus' time in the tomb. Given that Holy Saturday morning involves preparation for Easter, the Altar Guild gathering for this liturgy might be a good way to mark that time of preparation as sacred and set within the context of the Triduum.

The Great Vigil of Easter is unlike any other liturgy in the year; it's uniqueness is its distinction The color of the day is white or gold for glory, celebration, and light. This is the Feast of feasts in which we celebrate the passover of Jesus from death into life and our own passover from death into life in Holy Baptism. The service has four parts: the service of light, the vigil, the renewal of baptismal vows (or baptism), and Holy Eucharist.

A fire is kindled to drive away the darkness, and from the new fire the paschal candle is lit. The word *paschal* comes from the Latin and Greek word *pascha*, which means "Passover" From the earliest Christian practices a lit candle became a sign of the resurrection, passing over from the darkness of death to light in Christ. From this candle, the people light their own candles, and the church is filled with the light of Christ. The ancient hymn known as the *Exsultet* is sung, praising God for this night in which the ancient people of Israel were delivered from Egypt at the Red Sea, in which Christ rose from the dead, and in which we are baptized into his death and resurrection.

By the light of the new fire, passages from the Old Testament are read recounting the major events of salvation history. After each reading, we sing a psalm, anthem or hymn, and offer a prayer. The number varies from congregation to congregation: two are required, and up to nine may be read; the Exodus account at the Red Sea must be read to connect that ancient story of deliverance to our story of deliverance from sin and death to new life in Christ.

Having been reminded of the promises of salvation history, we may bring to the Font those who are to be baptized in keeping with the customs of the early Church when all were baptized at the Great Vigil of Easter. Or, we renew the promises of Baptism, by which we were adopted as children of God and made members of the Church. Either way, the Church rises from the waters of baptism, stands united in prayer before God, and the Risen Christ is made visible to the world. And, of course, our *Alleluia*, suppressed in Lent, is restored.

The first Eucharist of the Easter is now celebrated. As we have noted, each Eucharist is a repetition of the Easter Eucharist—this Eucharist. The letter of St. Paul to the Romans reminds us that in Baptism we have died with Christ in order that we may be raised with him (Romans 6:3-11). We hear Matthew's account of the empty tomb, when the risen Christ met the women and sent them to tell the others that he was risen from the dead as was promised. (Matthew 28:1-10) This liturgy begins the Great Fifty Days of Easter which culminate on the Day of Pentecost.

Eastertide

Celebrating the Resurrection of Jesus, this season is the oldest part of the Church Year and is derived directly from the fifty-day period in the Jewish calendar, which began with Passover and concluded with *Pentecost* (the Greek term for "fiftieth day"). Jesus' death and resurrection took place around Passover, and its completion— the empowering of the apostles by the Holy Spirit—took place on Pentecost, as we learn in the Acts of the Apostles. Easter and Pentecost were the earliest festivals and were both moved to Sundays, because of the early Church's reverence for the first day of the week as the Lord's Day, as discussed earlier.

The Paschal Candle burns in a prominent place in the church at every service during the season. Altar Guilds in our churches today should be grateful for the simplicity of most of our paschal candles: in some ancient basilicas the stand for the paschal candle was built as a permanent feature of the building's architecture. For centuries, Winchester Cathedral had a paschal candle that was over fifty feet tall! Today, in many places, the paschal candle is kept in a (reasonably sized) stand near the baptismal font.

Certain scriptural themes which highlight the meaning of the Resurrection have been part of the Church's tradition for many centuries. First, during Easter, we focus on readings from the Acts of the Apostles; this is a restoration of an ancient practice in the lectionary of the 1979 revision of the Book of Common Prayer. Acts is a description of the life of early Christian community, and it is characterized by the teachings of the Resurrection by the apostles. Second, the Sunday gospel readings tend to have similar themes each year: the Gospel reading for Second Sunday of Easter is always Jesus' appearance to Thomas; the third Sunday tells an account of a resurrection appearance in which Jesus shares a meal with his friends, signifying the eucharistic pattern that continues to this day; the Fourth Sunday is commonly called "Good Shepherd Sunday," when the Gospel reading reflects Jesus' relationship to us in the image of a shepherd; the fifth Sunday has readings which focus on Jesus' foretelling of his resurrection prior to his crucifixion, connecting his resurrection to his life and death; and, on the Sixth Sunday, Jesus describes, in some form, the results of our new life in Christ.

On the Thursday of the sixth week of Easter, we celebrate the Ascension of Jesus. Following the chronology of Luke's Gospel, the ascension falls on the fortieth day after the Resurrection. Though it is an important day and a vital part of the Easter story, sadly, many congregations no longer celebrate this principal feast.

Also, during the sixth week of Easter, some congregations keep Rogation Days. These date to the Middle Ages and connect our prayers for new life in Christ with the new life of the created world. For centuries, these days were marked by processions and the blessing of fields: before Earth Day, we had Rogation Days. Some parishes still mark Rogation with processions, garden-plantings and blessings, or other activities. The *Book of Occasional Services* provides a robust set of prayers, including options for use by parishes in urban centers.

On the Seventh Sunday of Easter: the Sunday after Ascension Day, we hear a portion of the "high-priestly prayer." This is the prayer Jesus prayed on the night before his death in John's Gospel—a prayer for the disciples and those who would come after them, down through the generations; in other words, a prayer for us.

Finally, the season of Easter is completed on the Day of Pentecost when we celebrate the gift of the Holy Spirit to the Church. While the color of the Easter season remains gold or white, on Pentecost, the color of the day changes to red. This symbolizes the tongues of fire and the gift of the Holy Spirit. The reading from the Acts of the Apostles tells of the coming of the Holy Spirit in tongues of fire, which enables the apostles to speak in many languages for the people gathered to hear and understand (Acts 2:1-11). The disunity created at the Tower of Babel is over with God reuniting humanity in Christ through the Holy Spirit. The day, a turning point on the Church calendar, focuses on us being empowered to be people of the resurrection and bearers of Christ's peace and love in the world for which Jesus was incarnated.

Season after the Pentecost

Here, we reach a major turning point in the Church year. Keeping in mind the two cycles described in the last chapter, we turn our focus to how we live as people of the paschal mystery of resurrection, in the world today. . In the months to come, we find ourselves learning how to be the living and visible sign of Christ .

The First Sunday after Pentecost is called Trinity Sunday. The focus here is not the celebration of a doctrine, but rather the celebration of our God whose self-revelation is as a community of love between Persons, whom we call Father, Son, and Holy Spirit. This community of love is the grounding of our life of faith.

Following Trinity Sunday, Sundays take their theme from the Gospel reading assigned for that day. During this period, we finish reading the Gospel assigned for the year, having started this in Advent and Epiphany. Several of the epistles, or letters to the early Churches, are read during this period. Depending on the chosen track, the Old Testament readings are either a semi-continuous telling of the history of God's people or are chosen to complement the themes of the Gospel reading each Sunday. In this way, the Season after the Pentecost affords us the chance to reflect on Scripture in an orderly and comprehensive way.

The liturgical color of this season is green, the sign of life and vegetation—a reminder that we are growing in our new life in the Risen Christ. The season is book-ended by two Sundays when white or gold vestments may be used: Trinity Sunday and the Last Sunday after Pentecost when we remember Christ the King or the Reign of Christ.

Two significant feasts fall within the time between Pentecost and the beginning of Advent: Transfiguration (August 6) and All Saints' Day (November 1). Both take precedence over Sundays. On Transfiguration, we recall the story of how Jesus' divinity was revealed in great light to Peter, James, and John on the mountain. Jesus and his disciples came down from the mountain to confront the powers of darkness that wish to destroy the light. Tthis feast reminds us that we, too, are called to do the same in our world.

All Saints' Day is the Church's celebration of the "great cloud of witnesses," all the holy people of God throughout the generations.

Some of these faithful are recognized by the Church and given days of remembrance and celebration; sometimes called "Saints." This day takes precedence over Sunday and can also be transferred to a Sunday if it falls during the week. Often it is combined with the Commemoration of the Faithful Departed, commonly called All Souls' Day (November 2) when we remember our loved ones who have died, as well as all those faithful people through whom we encountered Christ. These are often called "saints" but here with a lower case "s" since they are not officially recognized by the Church. Altar Guilds should take note of any special devotions or commemorations within your congregations.

The Season after Pentecost concludes on the Sunday before Advent begins. This Sunday is often called Christ the King Sunday, or more recently, the Reign of Christ. White or gold paraments and vestments may be used to signal glory and light since on this Sunday we celebrate Christ's universal rule over all creation and look forward to Christ's return bringing into fullness the vision of the perfect reign of God on earth.

And then, we begin again:

Almighty God, give us grace to cast away the works of darkness, and put on the armor of light, now in the time of this mortal life in which your Son Jesus Christ came to visit us in great humility; that in the last day, when he shall come again in his glorious majesty to judge both the living and the dead, we may rise to the life immortal; through him who lives and reigns with you and the Holy Spirit, one God, now and for ever. Amen. [211]

Advent to Advent, Sunday by Sunday, year after year, the story of God's redemption in Jesus' life, death, resurrection, and gift of the Holy Spirit is unfolded for us.

CHAPTER EIGHT

THE HOLY EUCHARIST: HISTORICAL DEVELOPMENT

At the Lamb's high feast we sing praise to our victorious King,
Who hath washed us in the tide flowing from his pierced side;
Praise we him, who love divine, gives his sacred Blood for wine,
Gives his Body for the feast, Christ the victim, Christ the priest.[1]

Shortly before my eighth birthday, I received my first Holy Communion. As we saw in a previous chapter, the prayer book shifted less than a decade earlier, and there was a move underway to disconnect the admittance to Communion from the Sacrament of Confirmation. I was part of one of the earliest "First Holy Communion" classes. It was understated; we went with our parents to receive Communion at the usual time and our names were printed in the bulletin as an acknowledgment that we had completed a course of study in Sunday School.

My parents gave me a copy of the Book of Common Prayer as a gift. While perhaps a seemingly strange gift to an eight-year-old, it is the prayer book that I use to this day when bringing Communion to the home-bound, anointing the sick, praying over those who are dying, and burying the dead. Very well worn, and in need of more than a few repairs, it brings me comfort to use that book because it reminds me of my earliest connections to the Eucharistic Table from which all Christian life and ministry flows.

I have no memory of the classes that preceded this *big day*. I do remember, though, talking a lot, in Sunday School about the Last

---

1. Latin, 1632; tr. Robert Campbell. *The Hymnal 1982*. (New York: Church Hymnal, 1985), 174.

Supper and that what we do in the Eucharist derives from that. So, as we begin our look at the historical development of the rite for Holy Eucharist as it appears in the Book of Common Prayer, that is where we will begin.

Last Supper

The institution of the Lord's Supper (or Holy Communion or the Eucharist or Mass) is recounted in the synoptic Gospels and St. Paul's First Letter to the Corinthians on the night before the Crucifixion. As devout Jews, Jesus and his disciples understood the significance of ritual, particularly the ritual of the Passover, in which what we call the Last Supper was set.

"This is the bread of the affliction which your fathers did eat when they came out of Egypt," or similar words would be familiar to Jesus' table guests at the Passover.[2] The host of the meal identifies some of the food with a part of the shared religious history, connecting God's actions in the past to the present. (We will see this in great detail in the post-Sanctus recalling of the redemptive acts of God in our own Eucharistic prayers.) Here, Jesus uses this ritual language of identification:

> While they were eating, Jesus took a loaf of bread, and after blessing it he broke it, gave it to the disciples, and said, "Take, eat; this is my body." Then he took a cup, and after giving thanks he gave it to them, saying, "Drink from it, all of you, for this is my blood of the covenant, which is poured out for many for the forgiveness of sins. I tell you, I will never again drink of this fruit of the vine until that day when I drink it new with you in my Father's kingdom." (Matthew 26:26-29)

Here the author of Matthew's Gospel does two things. First, Jesus identifies a piece of food not with a Divine historical action,

---

2. Price, Charles and Weil, Louis. *Liturgy for Living*. Revised Edition. (Harrisburg: Morehouse, 2000), 130.

but rather his own self. Second, he foreshadows not only his own death, resurrection, and ascension, but also the heavenly banquet to which we all are invited. The Gospel of Luke adds a key line for our understanding of the Eucharist:

> Then [Jesus] took a loaf of bread, and when he had given thanks he broke it and gave it to them, saying, "This is my body, which is given for you. *Do this in remembrance of me.*" And he did the same with the cup after supper, saying, "This cup that is poured out for you is the new covenant in my blood." (Luke 22:19-20, emphasis is mine)

To start, it is helpful to remember that the Gospels are based on the oral tradition of the apostles and reflect a custom that developed from the earliest days. Matthew, Mark , and Luke all present similar accounts of the Institution of the Lord's Supper. Luke, interestingly, adds the line "do this in remembrance of me," to emphasize the perpetual observance of this ritual first described by Paul.

> For I received from the Lord what I also handed on to you, that the Lord Jesus on the night when he was betrayed took a loaf of bread, and when he had given thanks, he broke it and said, "This is my body that is for you. Do this in remembrance of me." In the same way he took the cup also, after supper, saying, "This cup is the new covenant in my blood. Do this, as often as you drink it, in remembrance of me." For as often as you eat this bread and drink the cup, you proclaim the Lord's death until he comes. (1 Corinthians 11:23-26)

Paul's account in the Letter to the First Corinthians is crucial as it predates the synoptic gospels and provides a direct link the apostolic practice. Paul recounts Jesus' words, emphasizing the command to "do this in remembrance of me" and adding, "For as often as you eat this bread and drink the cup, you proclaim the

Lord's death until he comes." We can see that from the earliest days of the Church, the ritual of the Eucharist is clearly both a remembrance and a proclamation of God's salvific work in Jesus Christ.

The Early Church

> They devoted themselves to the apostles' teaching and fellowship, to the breaking of bread and the prayers. (Acts 2:42)

The *Acts of the Apostles* and early Christian writings provide insights into how the first Christians practiced the sacrament of the Eucharist. "Breaking of bread" is widely interpreted as a reference to the Lord's Supper and they—the first followers—embraced the sharing of this ritual meal as a central act of worship. It is clear that Jewish-Christians continued the practice of synagogue and Temple worship and, on the first day, gathered for prayer, recounted stories of Jesus, and shared a sacred meal.

The *Didache*, an early Christian document dating to the late first or early 2nd century, offers directions on Christian life and rituals, including the instruction: "on every Lord's Day—his special day—come together and break bread and give thanks."[3] It also provides admonitions, instructions, and prayers of thanksgiving reflecting this nascent Eucharistic practice as an integral part of Christian worship.

The dialogue between priest and people at the beginning of the Great Thanksgiving is found in the prayers of this time as well. Its roots are in the post-Biblical teachings and prescribed Jewish rituals of the Talmud which, in some form, Jesus and his disciples would most likely have used.

---

3. *The Didache*, XIV, trans. Cyril Richardson in *Sacraments and Worship: The Sources of Christian Theology*. Johnson, Maxwell, ed. (Louisville: Westminster, 2012), 183.

Host:　Let us give thanks unto our God.

Guests:　Blessed be the name of the Lord from this time forth forevermore.

Host:　With the assent of those present we will bless [the One] of Whose bounty we have partaken.

Guests:　Blessed be [the One] of Whose bounty we have partaken and through Whose goodness with live.[4]

We see evidence of this development in the Eucharistic prayers of the Antiochian rite and the prayers of St. John Chrysostom. In the early 3rd century, Hippolytus admonishes his readers that the Eucharistic prayer is to begin with this dialogue:

Bishop:　The Lord be with you.

All:　And with your spirit.

Bishop:　Up with your hearts.

All:　We have them with the Lord.

Bishop:　Let us give thanks to the Lord.

All:　It is fitting and right.[5]

While ritual and prayers, also called *anaphora*, were developing, so was Eucharistic theology. Thanksgiving for God's action in creation, in the exodus, in the words of the prophets, and in the incarnation of Jesus find their roots here. Also, the prayers of this period discuss the offering of our gifts and ourselves (*oblation*) as well as our participation in salvation through the Christian mystery connects our time and place in this act of remembering (*anamnesis*). During this period, the invocation of the Holy Spirit to sanctify and bless the gifts and people (*epiclesis*) appears prominently, as does the connection of the

---

4. As quoted in Price, Charles and Weil, Louis. *Liturgy for Living*. Revised Edition. (Harrisburg: Morehouse, 2000), 132.

5. The Anaphora of *The Apostolic Tradition*, trans. Geoffrey J. Cumming, in *Hippolytus: A Text for Students* (Bramcote: Grove, 1976) in *Sacraments and Worship: The Sources of Christian Theology*. Johnson, Maxwell, ed. (Louisville: Westminster, 2012), 194.

ritual act to the communion of Saints. All of this should sound very familiar to the observant Episcopalian!

One other key theological development was the assertion of the real presence of Christ in the Eucharist. Ignatius of Antioch, a prominent early Christian bishop and martyr under the Roman Emperor Trajan, wrote several letters around 110 CE, emphasizing the importance of the Eucharist. In his letter to the Smyrnaeans, he challenges the heresy of the Docetists, who did not admit the Eucharist as "the flesh of our Savior Jesus Christ."[6] This underscores the early belief in the real presence of Christ in the Eucharist, which is rooted in the Bread of Life discourse in John's Gospel which records Jesus as saying: "Those who eat my flesh and drink my blood have eternal life, and I will raise them up on the last day." (6:54)

Similarly, Justin Martyr, writing in the mid-2nd century, provides a detailed description of the Eucharist in his *First Apology*, which is still discernible in several rites today. Justin explains that the bread and wine, through prayer, become the body and blood of Christ. What this means will continue to develop and centuries later will become a great point of contention of the Reformation.

The Rise of a Systematic Theology

It is impossible, in this short volume, to provide an extensive history of the development of the Eucharistic rite so our discussion will continue to move rapidly (depending on your point of view) through the centuries, touching on points pertinent to our understanding of the Eucharistic rite as it appears today in the Book of Common Prayer.

During the Middle Ages, Eucharistic ritual practice and theology was further expanded and systematized. Highly enlarged rites emerged over the centuries, as did a pattern with which we are mostly familiar

---

6. Ignatius of Antioch, *Letters (c.115)*, trans. Cyril Richardson, in *Sacraments and Worship: The Sources of Christian Theology*. Johnson, Maxwell, ed. (Louisville: Westminster, 2012), 184.

in most forms of the Great Thanksgiving today: Sursum Corda, Preface, Sanctus, Post-Sanctus and Epiclesis, Institution Narrative, Anamnesis and Oblation, and Doxology.

In the Medieval period, we also see the development of the theological concept of transubstantiation. The Fourth Lateran Council (1215) concluded:

> In [the Church universal] Jesus himself is both priest and sacrifice, whose body and blood are truly contained in the sacrament of the altar under the species of bread and wine by the transubstantiation of bread into body and wine into blood through divine power: that through the perfecting of the mystery of unity we receive of him from himself, that which he received from us.[7]

Our focus here is on transubstantiation; however, it would be good to keep in mind for later discussion: "we receive from [Christ of Christ's-self] that which [Christ] received from us." Sound familiar? To say it another way, the bread and wine which we offer are returned to us as *the gifts of God for the people of God*.

Thomas Aquinas (1225-1274) was a Dominican monk and priest, philosopher, and theologian and probably the greatest thinker and writer of the Medieval period Aquinas' doctrine of transubstantiation, articulated in his *Summa Theologica,* advances the idea that the substance, or true essence, of bread and wine becomes in substance Christ's body and blood, while the accidents (appearances) of bread and wine remain. Coinciding with this theological concept are two other practices: 1) the focus on the sinfulness of the recipient of communion and the need for ritual purity to receive the sacrament; and 2) the development of adulation of the sacrament in place of

---

7. Fourth Lateran Council (1215) from *Enchiridion Symbolorum Definitinuem et Declarationium,* ed. Henry Denzinger and Adolf Schonmetzer, 33 ed. (Freiburg: Herder, 1965) in *Sacraments and Worship: The Sources of Christian Theology.* Johnson, Maxwell, ed. (Louisville: Westminster, 2012), 225-6.

the sharing of the sacrament by all, for if this is the "actual" body of Christ on earth, then gazing upon it and adoring it is an appropriate act of worship.

The idea of transubstantiation became deeply embedded in the prayers and doctrine of the Church. The liturgy also now included highly elaborate and complex rituals for the celebration of the Holy Eucharist which the reduced the laity to mere viewers of a performance. They now gazed upon the sacrament in adoration rather than engaged as participants in the liturgy. This provided the atmospheric conditions in the Church suitable to yield a great storm and the first wind of that storm was Martin Luther.

The Protestant Reformation

Martin Luther (1483-1546) was a German Augustinian priest, theologian, and hymnwriter. He was the seminal figure of the Protestant Reformation, known for his *Ninety-Five Theses*, which he mailed to the archbishop and, according to the customs of the university, posted on doors of churches in Wittenberg, Germany on or about October 31, 1517. In this work, he detailed, out of concern for the Church, the reforms he believed necessary. The reproduction of this pamphlet, along with ensuing debates between Luther and the hierarchy of the Church, led to Luther's excommunication in 1521.

In Luther's writings, he condemns the elaborate and complex practices and theology of the Roman Mass while maintaining the concept of the real presence of Christ in the Holy Eucharist, which he believes is Christ's gift to the Church. In *Babylonian Captivity of the Church*, Luther makes the following points:

> The *first captivity of this sacrament*…concerns its substance or completeness, which the tyranny of Rome has wrestled from us….The sacrament does not belong to the priests but to all [people]. The priests are not lords, but servants in duty bound

to administer both kinds to those who desire them, as often as they desire them....

The *second captivity of this sacrament* [is transubstantiation].... It is not necessary in the sacrament that the bread and wine be transubstantiated and that Christ be contained under their accidents in order that the real body and real blood may be present. But both remain there at the same time....

The *third captivity of this sacrament* is by far the most wicked abuse of all.... The holy sacrament has been turned into mere merchandize, a market, and a profit-making business...[8]

The great scholasticism movement of the Middle Ages either backfired or triumphed depending on your perspective in the early 16th century. Ulrich Zwingli, John Calvin, Balthsar Hübmaier, and others continued, refined and expanded on Luther's ideas, writing systematic theologies on Eucharistic Reformation as well as other reformations needed in the Church, many making their breaks with the Church of Rome, by choice or by excommunication. This continental reformation in the Western Church had influence on English Reformation and the development, as we have seen, of the Book of Common Prayer.

English Reformation

As the Protestant Reformation brought significant changes to the theology and practice of the Eucharist, in England a middle way was being sought between Roman Catholicism and the new reformed Churches. As we saw in Chapter 5, the first Book of Common Prayer in 1549 reflected this *via media* approach: The complex and elaborate rites are simplified; there is no elevation or showing of the

8. Martin Luther, *The Babylonian Captivity of the Church* (1520), A.T.W. Steinhauser, Frederick Ahrens, and Abdel Wentz, trans. In *Sacraments and Worship: The Sources of Christian Theology*. Johnson, Maxwell, ed. (Louisville: Westminster, 2012), 228-9.

sacrament to the people, that it may not be gazed upon but received; the sacrament is received in both kinds; and Archbishop Cranmer's Eucharistic theology rejects transubstantiation, though emphasizing the real presence of Christ in the Eucharist.

For some, the prayer book changed too much, and it was virtually ignored. For others, the prayer book changed far too little and actual riots broke out where altars were removed and statues torn down. The more significant change in the Eucharistic rite came with the 1552 Book of Common Prayer. Here Cranmer does not attempt to soothe the catholic wing. Rather, we see the influence of the Reformation on his thinking.

First, the use of vestments (chasuble or cope) is prohibited, whereas before it was directed. Second, the rite is simplified further, and the more fulsome Eucharistic Prayer of 1549 is reduced to the "Prayer of Consecration," eliminating the *anamnesis* and epiclesis and focusing the prayer on the sacrifice of Christ on the Cross and a much-simplified institution narrative commemorating the Last Supper. Third, the words of administration of Communion change from: "The Body of our Lord Christ which was given for thee, preserve thy body and soul unto everlasting" to "Take and eat this in remembrance that Christ died for thee and feed on him in thy heart, by faith with thanksgiving." Christ is present only spiritually in our hearts by this commemoration of the Last Supper. Finally, any reference to "offering," other than that of the collection of alms, is eliminated. The bread and wine are prepared on the holy table before the service and there is no mention of the people offering anything to God. In this prayer book, God acts, and the people passively receive and respond.

Later prayer books try to strike a balance between the extremes of the medieval liturgies and reformed practices. The Elizabethan prayer book (1559) was seen as a peacemaking book: vestments were again permissible and the words of administration of Communion combined the 1549 and 1552 ideas, striking a balance between emphasizing the real presence of Christ in the sacrament and focusing on the presence of Christ in our hearts and memory alone. This remains an option in our prayer book to this day and is most obvious in the words of administration in Rite One: "The Body of our Lord Jesus Christ, which was given for thee, preserve thy body and soul unto everlasting life. Take and eat this in remembrance that Christ died for thee, and feed on him in thy heart by faith, with thanksgiving." [338]

The 1604 and 1662 prayer books made minor changes, mostly around the modernization of language and rubrics for the conduct of the service that reflected a more Puritan church culture. A whiff of a theological change around "offering" came in 1662, when the bread and wine are placed on the altar at the time of the prayer of consecration rather than before the service begins.

A Prayer Book of the Episcopal Church

That hint of a change was less subtle in 1789. As we discussed in Chapter 5, the first Book of Common Prayer for use in the newly founded United States of America was a combination of the 1662 Book of Common Prayer of the Church of England and the Scottish Communion rite. To the Eucharistic liturgy was added Jesus' Summary of the Law after the recitation of the Ten Commandments as well as the Oblation ("offering") and Invocation of the Holy Spirit (*epiclesis*) within the Prayer of Consecration. Of this change, it has been said:

> The reappearance of the Oblation marks a significant step in recovering an explicit statement in the liturgy of what the eucharistic action is: the congregation's offering of bread and wine in thankful remembrance of all God has done for us through Christ. The Invocation of the Spirit simply brings into sharper focus material that has always been in the eucharist prayer in English books, before the account of the Supper.[9]

---

9. Price, Charles and Weil, Louis. *Liturgy for Living*. Revised Edition. (Harrisburg: Morehouse, 2000), 60.

An interesting aside: the first editions of the prayer book in the Episcopal Church make no reference to vestments or ornamentation in the sanctuary. This left it to the custom and practice of individual congregations and most opted for a more Puritan approach with unvested clergy and no decorations or paraments. What might seem odd to us today is that there were great debates and even ecclesiastical trials related to the use of vestments, paraments, flowers, and other decorations into the late 1800s.

Those of us familiar with the current prayer book and common liturgical practices will find the groundwork for this laid in the liturgical movements of the 19th century. As we have seen elsewhere in our discussions, two forces pressured the Episcopal Church in late-1800s: the Oxford Movement and societal changes. The appreciation for and revival of medieval liturgical practices began at Oxford University in England and was led by John Henry Newman, E.B. Pusey, and John Keble. The re-discovered richness of these traditions spread quickly in Anglicanism and led to an increased desire to apply them in the liturgies of the Episcopal Church.

On the other side, industrialization and urbanization, along with growing tolerance of religious pluralism were key features of life in the late 1800s in the United States. This led the more liberal wing of the Episcopal Church to call for the shortening of services because of employment demands of the working-class and greater flexibility in the use of the prayer book to accommodate the diversity of faith practices of new immigrants.

In the 1892 and 1928 prayer book revisions, little changed in the Eucharistic rite. However, it was clear that significant change was inevitable. Two key things happened at General Convention in 1928 that signaled the Church was prepared for the change. First, the prayer book rubrics were amended to read that along with the alms, "the Priest shall then *offer*, and shall place upon the Holy Table the Bread and Wine." Oblation resumed a greater role.

And the second, and probably the most significant act of the 1928 General Convention, was to create the Standing Commission on Liturgy and Church Music (then called Standing Liturgical Commission). As we saw in Chapter 5, the role of this commission was to review the scholarship of the liturgical renewal movement along with ecumenical texts to create new and trial liturgies. This process eventually led to today's prayer book.

Finally, back to our questions about transubstantiation, consubstantiation, simple memorial, or real presence: which is it? Anglican Eucharistic theology can still be best summed up in the purported words of Queen Elizabeth I:

[Jesus] was the Word that spake it,
He took the bread and brake it;
And what that Word did make it,
I do believe and take it.[10]

---

10. As found in Price, Charles and Weil, Louis. *Liturgy for Living*. Revised Edition. (Harrisburg: Morehouse, 2000), 154.

CHAPTER NINE

THE HOLY EUCHARIST: TODAY'S THEOLOGY

The Eucharist is the entrance of the Church into the joy of its Lord. And to enter into that joy, so as to be a witness to it in the world, is indeed the very calling of the Church, its essential leitouriga, the sacrament by which it "becomes what it is."

Alexander Schmemann[1]

G rowing up in my church, Sunday School was between the two services so that the children, who are in fact members of the whole community, could attend Holy Eucharist. I may not have understood all that was being read, said, or prayed and I may have even been a bit bored. Yet, even as a young child, the rhythm, pattern, words, and music of the liturgy enveloped me, so that today the Eucharistic feast is deeply familiar and the liturgy comforts, challenges, and inspires me.

Ordo: Proclaim and Respond

This underlying pattern that enveloped me as a child is called the *ordo*, the theological concept that is the foundation for liturgy. Of *ordo*, James Farwell writes this:

If a sentence can say something only because it follows the grammatical rules of the language in which it is written, so the liturgy—the things we say, do, and sing, and the movements

---

1. Schmemann, Alexander. *For the Life of the Word* (Crestwood: St. Vladimar's, 1976), 26.

and gestures we make—is possible only as it unfolds by the "rules" of the ordo.[2]

For Farwell, the ordo or deep grammar of the liturgy is proclamation and response. On its most obvious level, we begin with the proclamation of the Word of God—the Liturgy of the Word—and we respond with Holy Communion—or the Liturgy of the Table. This is not limited to just looking at the two parts of the whole celebration of the Holy Eucharist, but this pattern applies also within these two requisite parts.

Within the Liturgy of the Word, we begin by hearing the Word of God proclaimed in the lessons from Scripture, the psalm, and the sermon. Hearing the Word of God proclaimed and being reminded of God's goodness and grace, we respond by affirming our faith through the Nicene Creed, offering our prayers for the world that God created, redeemed, and sustains, and acknowledging in the confession that we ourselves have fallen short of the life which we are to live as those created in the image and likeness of God.

Having been put in mind of God's forgiveness, our liturgy moves us to the Eucharistic Prayer or the Great Thanksgiving. In that prayer, salvation history is proclaimed and we respond by sharing Communion with one another and going into the world to continue Christ's ministry as witnesses to the love of God which we have heard proclaimed. Turn the microscope a notch more: in the first part of the Eucharistic Prayer, God is praised for acts in creation and salvation history and we respond by calling God's blessing upon the bread and the wine and ourselves that all might become gifts of God and witnesses of God's love.

As we discussed in our chapter on liturgical theology, God acts first and we respond, so here, in our celebration of the Holy Eucharist, proclamation precedes response. This is the *ordo*, or deep grammar,

---

2. Farwell, James. *The Liturgy Explained*. (New York: Morehouse, 2013), 15.

of the liturgy of the Eucharist—and even more so, the liturgy of our lives. Farwell concludes:

> Perhaps, too, in the end the entire liturgy is proclamation: the gathering of the people of God is from the beginning to the end of the worship of God from whom all life flows, whose worship inspires and empowers the people of God to respond. The form of that response is to return to the world and engage again, by God's grace and help, in the building of the kingdom that is ultimately God's work.[3]

Building on this deep pattern of worship, a second level of *ordo* exists in our prayer book and this is around what makes "common prayer" throughout Anglicanism today. What makes our prayer "common" is not that Anglicans around the world say the same words Sunday to Sunday, because of course we don't, given the rich variation of prayer books reflecting the diversity of local language and culture. What makes it "common" is what the 1995 International Anglican Liturgical Consultation called a shared liturgical tradition and a fivefold sequence in the Eucharist. This sequence is:

1. Gathering of God's People
2. Proclaiming and Receiving the Word of God
3. Prayers of the People
4. Celebrating at the Lord's Table
5. Going out as God's people.[4]

As we begin our look at the liturgy for the Holy Eucharist within the Book of Common Prayer, we will examine it using this fivefold sequence of Anglican unity. An effort has been made to demonstrate this pattern using broadly the authorized texts of the prayer book.

---

3. Ibid, 18.

4. Meyers, Ruth and Mitchell, Leonel. *Praying Shapes Believing: A Theological Commentary on the Book of Common Prayer.* (New York: Seabury, 2016), 150.

Gathering of God's People

> We the Lord's people, heart and voice uniting, Praise him
> who called us out of sin and darkness in his own light That he
> might anoint us a royal priesthood. In the Lord's service bread
> and wine are offered That Christ may take them, bless them,
> break and give them to all his people His own life imparting,
> food everlasting.[5]

Sometimes called the entrance or gathering rite, this opening part
of the liturgy is not named in the Book of Common Prayer. The
prayer book actually assigns no formal entrance, however, it is logical
to assume that liturgical ministers need to get to their places. A
gathering hymn, anthem, or song should be more than just cover for
liturgical ministers to get into place. This hymn has a much deeper
meaning: it unites the congregation so that together they as the
Body of Christ assembled can respond as one in praise of God. The
Opening Acclamation then is an extension of that hymn: "Blessed
be the one, holy, and living God." [EOW, 50]. The first words of the
liturgy, whether a hymn or the acclamation, are in praise of God. .

Following the Opening Acclamation, for which there are seasonal
options both within the prayer book and *Enriching our Worship*, the
Collect for Purity is often said. This collect has been used since 1549
as a preparatory prayer that voices the sentiments with which all
should approach worship: "Cleanse the thoughts of our hearts by the
inspiration of your Holy Spirit, that we may perfectly love you, and
worthily magnify your holy name." [355] A hymn of praise follows,
usually the *Gloria in excelsis Deo* or other festive hymn. The *Kyrie* or
Trisagion are less festal options and appropriate during penitential
seasons.

The Collect of the Day concludes this gathering rite in our liturgy.
This prayer "collects" the individual prayers of the people gathered

---

5. Bowers, John. "We the Lord's people." (New York: Church Hymnal, 1985), 51.

and focuses them on a theme of the day. The collects are prescribed by the prayer book. Many of the ones used today are modernizations of those first collects used in English in 1549 and are rooted in the ancient liturgies of the Church. These prayers unite us with fellow Episcopalians and Anglicans throughout the whole Church and they coincide with the lessonsthat are to follow.

Proclaiming and Receiving the Word of God

> [Jesus] stood up to read [in the synagogue] and the scroll of the prophet Isaiah was given to him. He unrolled the scroll and found the place where it was written: "The Spirit of the Lord is upon me, because he has anointed me to bring good news to the poor. He has sent me to proclaim release to the captives and recovery of sight to the blind, to set free those who are oppressed, to proclaim the year of the Lord's favor." And he rolled up the scroll, gave it back to the attendant, and sat down. The eyes of all in the synagogue were fixed on him. Then he began to say to them, "Today this scripture has been fulfilled in your hearing." (Luke 4:16-21)

The assigned lessons, or readings, from Scripture follow a three-year cycle. Since 2007, the Episcopal Church has used the *Revised Common Lectionary*, which is shared across several Churches around the world. For Sundays and Major Feasts three lessons are usually assigned: an Old Testament lesson, a New Testament lesson, and a Gospel lesson. As we discussed in a previous chapter, there are two cycles for the year—Paschal and Incarnational—and readings that fall within those cycles reflect the theological themes of that season.

During the Seasons after Epiphany and Pentecost, sometimes called Ordinary Time, we hear lessons from one of the synoptic gospels (Matthew, Mark, Luke). During the Season after the Pentecost, there are two tracks from which to choose: 1) the semi-continuous option, which reads large sections of the Old Testament mostly in order and addresses the concern about using Hebrew Scriptures simply to amplify, possibly out of context, the New Testament; and 2) passages from the Old Testament related closely to the lesson assigned from the Gospels.

The prayer book allows for the assigned psalm, or a hymn, anthem or silence after each reading. Remnants of the medieval rites are found in the terms we use. The response to is the first lessonis sometimes called the Gradual from the Latin word *gradus*, referring to "the step" from where the response was once led. The Sequence, often a hymn, is then sung after the Epistle and before the Gospel.

The Holy Gospel holds a place of honor and is read by the deacon, or priest in absence of one, from the pulpit, lectern, or amid the congregation. The Gospel procession is symbolic of the Word coming into the midst of the people. The custom of standing for this lesson acknowledges the reality behind it: that these are the very words of Jesus.

No hymn or anthem should come between the proclamation of the Gospel and the expounding on the Gospel in the Sermon. When present, the bishop preaches. While priests have been ordained to preach, in some dioceses, deacons may be permitted to, as well as licensed lay people. The sermon is an essential part of the liturgy, and its purpose is to break open the Word of God, making it relevant for the faithful today.

The Creed and Prayers of the People

A sign of unity of the Church, and a reminder of our baptismal covenants, the recitation of the Nicene Creed was introduced in the Eastern rites in the 6th century and in the Western rites in the 11th century. Often confused with swearing allegiance, *credo*, the Latin word from which we derive creed, can be translated as "put one's trust in." The Creed then is the faithful response, the singing or reciting of our faith in God, offered by the assembly to hearing the proclaimed Word of God. It is to be sung or said on Sundays and Major Feasts.

. In 1785, it was proposed to eliminate the Nicene Creed from the rites of the prayer book in the newly formed Episcopal Church. However, to maintain unity with the Church of England, it was agreed that leaving the creedal statement would appease the concerns of the bishops in England who were seeking to restore the relationship between the two churches in this Anglican tradition.

The Episcopal Church allows the use of the more inclusive translation of the Nicene Creed from *Enriching our Worship* in place of the one in the Book of Common Prayer. The translation in *Enriching our Worship* also eliminates the *filioque*, which says the Holy Spirit proceeds from the Father *and the Son*; this is in keeping with the original Greek and the custom of the Eastern rite churches.

It is probably helpful to note here that the Church does not allow the use of other Creeds. The faith of the Church is best expressed through our liturgy and, if the creed is eliminated, such as it is on a weekday or other occasions, the faith of the Church is expressed through the Great Thanksgiving and the entire liturgy itself; no additional statements are necessary.

Having heard the Word of God proclaimed and singing our faith, our prayers continue with the Prayers of the People. The deacon, who by ordination "interpret[s] to the Church the needs, concerns, and hopes of the world," leads these prayers when present. [543]

The Prayers of the People are the opportunity for the dynamic corporate prayer of the assembly and the prayer book allows the utmost flexibility here provided that certain topics are covered: the Universal Church, the Nation, the welfare of the world, the concerns of the local community, those who suffer and those in any trouble, and the departed. [359] This edition of the Book of Common Prayer has retained in Rite One the prayer for the Whole State of Christ's

Church, which first appeared 1549 within the eucharistic anaphora, and has offered six forms in Rite Two. In the latter order, these are guidelines and examples: the prayers of the people should be the most changing, and relevant part of the liturgy. Plenty of resources are available to help craft contemporary and timely corporate prayers.

Concluding the section of the prayers is the Confession of Sin, if not part of the earlier entrance or preparatory rite. This ritual act "is the verbalization of that private personal confession that each Christian has already made and is a recognition of our participation in the sinfulness of the world."[6] As part of our response to having heard the Word of God proclaimed, we acknowledge that we have failed to live the life commended to us in our baptisms and Scripture and we are also put in mind of God's forgiveness through Christ by the absolution offered by the bishop or priest. And, so we respond again by…

Celebrating at the Lord's Table

So when you are offering your gift at the altar, if you remember that your brother or sister has something against you, leave your gift there before the altar and go; first be reconciled to your brother or sister, and then come and offer your gift. (Matthew 5:23-24)

The Peace is a solemn liturgical ritual. Save the conversations for Coffee Hour! This is the final action of the Liturgy of the Word and the first action of the Liturgy of the Table. As it binds the two parts of the liturgy, our proclamation and response, here those who greet each other will become one in Christ through the sacrament of the altar.

---

6. Meyers, Ruth and Mitchell, Leonel. *Praying Shapes Believing: A Theological Commentary on the Book of Common Prayer*. (New York: Seabury, 2016), 161.

Offertory

Holy Communion continues with the offering of the bread and wine, placing them on the altar, and preparing the Holy Table for the Eucharistic feast A hymn or anthem may be sung as "representatives of the congregation bring the people's offerings of bread and wine, and money or other gifts, to the deacon or celebrant." [361] You will remember that this is a key change in our prayer books and part of our discussion of *oblation*.

Eucharistic Dialogue

The Great Thanksgiving then begins with the Eucharistic dialogue, often called the *sursum corda* after the Latin text for "lift up your hearts." The dialogue between the presider and people recalls the ancient table prayers of the Jewish faith and invites the people to join as full participants in, and not merely witnesses of, the Eucharistic Prayer. In the 4th century, Cyril of Jerusalem commanded us to "lay aside the cares of this life," to keep our hearts focused on God. Over 1300 years later, John Calvin said that only when we raise our hearts and minds will our souls be nourished.[7] In other words, God is not brought down to us, but we are called beyond ourselves, lifting up our hearts.

The presider's bidding for us to give thanks invites all into this earthly and heavenly action of the Eucharist. Hereafter, the presider acts in the name of the Church and proclaims the prayer on behalf of all assembled.

Preface

Following the opening dialogue, all prayers begin with giving thanks to God, the "creator of heaven and earth." [361] Proper prefaces may be used in most prayers to connect the prayer to the season or occasion. (Eucharistic prayers C, D, EOW 2 and 3 do not provide

---

7. Ibid, 168.

for this option, though in some cases a creative liturgist can carefully insert an appropriate preface.) Prayers C, D and all three options in *Enriching our Worship* present the most extensive thanksgiving for creation: "From before time you made ready the creation. Your Spirit moved over the deep and brought all things into being: sun, moon, and stars; earth, winds, and waters; and every living thing." [EOW, 60]

Eucharistic Prayer 1 from Rite One is based on Cranmer's 1549 prayer and does not mention creation at all. This reflects the medieval focus on atonement in the prayer of consecration unlike most of the earlier prayers of the Church.

Sanctus & Benedictus

The Eucharist is not simply the action of a particular congregation but of the whole Church, even the whole of creation. The worship of God is a cosmic act that this congregation in this time and place now joins. And so, "we join with Saints and Angels in the chorus of praise that rings through eternity." [EOW, 60] The *Sanctus* (Latin for "holy") references the great hymns before God's throne in heaven in both Isaiah.

> I saw the Lord sitting on a throne, high and lofty, and the hem of his robe filled the temple. Seraphs were in attendance above him; each had six wings: with two they covered their faces, and with two they covered their feet, and with two they flew. And one called to another and said, "Holy, holy, holy is the Lord of hosts; the whole earth is full of his glory." The pivots on the thresholds shook at the voices of those who called, and the house filled with smoke. (Isaiah 6:1-4)

As an aside, the *Benedictus*—"blessed is he who comes in the name of the Lord" [362]—references Jesus' triumphal entry into Jerusalem. It only reappeared in 1979 after being removed in prayer books from 1552 on because it was thought to refer to the coming of Christ into the eucharistic elements (and it remains optional in Rite One).

Post-Sanctus

Following the *Sanctus*, prayers are now offered in thanksgiving for our redemption throughout salvation history and in the atoning life and death of Jesus Christ. Any thanksgiving for our redemption in previous prayer books connected it solely to Christ's death, where Jesus offered the only offering that could and should be offered for the sins of the world; a response to the Medieval theological idea that the Eucharist completes it or offers it anew.

Eucharistic Prayer A presents a visual for us rather than any technical theological or language around the atoning life and death: "He stretched out his arms upon the cross and offered himself in obedience to your will, a perfect sacrifice for the whole world." [362] Eucharistic Prayer B expands our thanksgiving for God's salvific actions throughout history gives thanks to God "for the goodness and love which [God has] made known to us in creation; in the calling of Israel... in [the] Word spoken through the prophets; and... in the Word made flesh, Jesus." [368] *Enriching our Worship* Eucharistic Prayer 1 connects our story more specifically to the arc of salvation history referencing Abraham and Sarah, delivery from slavery in Egypt, and the redemption being brought to completion in Jesus. [EOW, 58]

The arc of salvation history points to the Incarnation. Eucharistic Prayer B says: "For in these last days [God] sent [Jesus] to be incarnate from the Virgin Mary, to be the Savior and Redeemer of the word."[368] *Enriching our Worship 2* gives thanks to God who "looked with favor upon Mary, [God's] willing servant, that she might conceive and bear a son, Jesus the holy child of God." [EOW, 61] Note here that Mary is portrayed as a "willing servant" and an active participant in the Incarnation.

Jesus' life of ministering to outcasts and sinners, healing the sick, and proclaiming good news is explicitly tied to the salvation history in some of our prayers as well. Prayer D, the most fulsome of the Eucharistic prayers in our prayer book, says it this way:

> Incarnate by the Holy Spirit, born of the Virgin Mary, he lived as one of us, yet without sin. To the poor he proclaimed the good news of salvation; to prisoners, freedom; to the sorrowful, joy. To fulfill your purpose he gave himself up to death; and, rising from the grave, destroyed death, and made the whole creation new. [374]

Words of Institution

Our thanksgiving for redemption is linked now to this celebration of the Holy Eucharist, which is done at Jesus' command. That bridge is expressed well here:

> *"We thank you that* on the night before he died for us, Jesus took bread, and when he had given thanks to you, he broke it, gave it to his friends and said: Take, eat, this is my Body, broken for you. Do this for the remembrance of me." [EOW, 64, emphasis is mine]

In some ways, as we remember, it is as if we are at the table with Jesus, though it is not a re-creation of that moment. Rather, in this meal, we encounter Jesus not as the disciples did in person, but as the resurrected and ascended Christ, who is both present and absent. Farwell notes:

> "in a certain way, the absence of Jesus is important to his presence in us, the assembly. Jesus must 'ascend' to God, making space for the community to continue his work in the assurance of its accomplishment and being freed from the limitations of space and time so that he is present in all places and times as God's Living Word has, in fact, always been."[8]

---

8. Farwell, James. *The Liturgy Explained.* (New York: Morehouse, 2013), 41.

Many liturgical customaries will point us to this being the moment of consecration, or the key moment in our Eucharistic prayer or liturgy, especially if we believe that the celebrant is acting *in persona Christi* (as the person of Christ). The rubrics of the Book of Common Prayer indicate here that the bread and wine are to be held or touched. Elevation, genuflection, or adoration are all local not universal customs, and find their rich theological roots throughout liturgical history.

Anamnesis

We often use the word memorial in a way that reflects the act of thinking about things of the past, as a sort of nostalgia. Here, rather, we become participants in the events of salvation, not as recounting of historical events, but as present reality in our lives.

> Father, *we now celebrate this memorial of our redemption.* Recalling Christ's death and his descent among the dead, proclaiming his resurrection and ascension to your right hand, awaiting his coming in glory; and *offering to you, from the gifts you have given us,* this bread and this cup…[374, emphasis is mine]

Oblation

The offering of our gifts to God and our remembrance connects past redemption with future promises at this moment. Here we can turn to the words of Cranmer from 1549, preserved in Rite One:

> Wherefore, O Lord and heavenly Father, according to the institution of thy dearly beloved Son our Savior Jesus Christ, *we, thy humble servants, do celebrate and make here before thy divine Majesty, with these thy holy gifts, which we now offer unto thee, the memorial thy Son hath commanded us to make…*

And here *we offer and present unto thee, O Lord, our selves, our souls and bodies, to be a reasonable, holy, and living sacrifice unto thee*; humbly beseeching thee that we, and all others who shall be partakers of this Holy Communion, *may worthily receive the most precious Body and Blood of thy Son Jesus Christ*, be filled with thy grace and heavenly benediction, and made one body with him, that he may dwell in us, and we in him. [335-36, emphasis is mine]

Epiclesis

The *epiclesis* is the invocation of the Holy Spirit upon the eucharistic gifts and often upon the eucharistic assembly. Sometimes this moment is described as the point of consecration; for example, in *Enriching our Worship* Eucharistic Prayer 3, it is obviously the zenith of the prayer. Little can be gained, however, by trying to figure out the moment of consecration; the prayer book presumes the entire prayer is consecratory. Most of our prayers follow the ancient Eastern rite practices of the *epiclesis* following the words of the institution; however, Eucharistic Prayer C, Form 1, and EOW Form A, place the *epiclesis* before the words of institution.

Heavenly Banquet

Our eucharistic prayers all imply that this meal is a foretaste of the heavenly banquet and offer the eschatological hope of sharing in the communion of the Saints. In Eucharistic Prayer B we pray, "bring us to that heavenly country where, with all your saints, we may enter the everlasting heritage of your sons and daughters." [369] *Enriching our Worship* Prayer 2 extends this imagery saying, "in the fullness of time bring us with all your saints, from every tribe and language and people and nation, to feast at the banquet prepared from the foundation of the world." [EOW, 62] Again, our celebration of the

Eucharist is linked beyond ourselves to the whole Body of Christ, in all times and in all places.

Doxology and the Lord's Prayer

Called the "doxology," the final part of the prayer is offered through Jesus with the invocation of the Holy Trinity. Doxology comes from the Latin and Greek words that mean speaking of the glory of God. The Great Amen that punctuates the conclusion of the prayer is the assent of the people to that which has been offered on their behalf. The Lord's Prayer which follows then binds us together and expresses our unity with one another in Christ.

Sharing of Communion

While primarily a utilitarian action, the breaking of bread, or fraction, that follows the spoken prayers has ritual significance. From 1552 on, the breaking of the bread was within the prayer itself but was moved in 1979. When the bread is broken within the prayer, it implies that the priest is acting out the part of Jesus, who took bread and broke it. It's placement here should remove that imagery and places the emphasis on Christ's presence both in the bread and wine and in the sharing of the eucharistic feast.

The prayer book rubric is clear that silence follows before any anthem or invitation is sung or said. It is in that silence that we can reflect on all that has been prayed before and we can see ourselves upon that altar offering our life to become the body of Christ for the world. Augustine, in preaching to the newly baptized, pointed them to the altar, saying:

> If it's you that are the body of Christ and its members, it's the mystery meaning you that has been placed on the Lord's table...It is to what you are that you reply *Amen*, and by so replying you express your assent... So be a member of the

body of Christ, in order to make that *Amen* true… Be what you see, and receive what you are.[9]

A *confractorium*, or Fraction Anthem, may be sung or said to connects us to the Paschal mystery in our sharing of the food of the reign of God. Here the invitation to communion—"the gifts of God for the people of God"—is offered, and we remember the teaching of the Fourth Lateran Council: "that through the perfecting of the mystery of unity *we receive of him from himself, that which he received from us.*"[10]

The people then receive "the body of Christ, the bread of heaven" and "the blood of Christ, the cup of salvation." The language from previous prayer books is now optional: "feed on him in your hearts by faith with thanksgiving." [365] Thus, the emphasis is placed back on the real presence of Christ and our participation in this mystery.

Going out as God's People

The Eucharist is the entrance of the Church into the joy of its Lord. And to enter into that joy, *so as to be a witness to it in the world*, is indeed the very calling of the Church, its essential *leitouriga*, the sacrament by which it "becomes what it is."

Alexander Schmemann[11]

The Book of Common Prayer leaves little to do after the reception of communion. Having encountered God proclaimed and acting in Word and Sacrament, we should be prepared to respond, to go into the

---

9. Augustine, "Sermon 272," in *The Works of St. Augustine*, Vol III/7, trans Edmund Hill (New Rochelle: New City, 1993) in Farwell, James. *The Liturgy Explained*. (New York: Morehouse, 2013), 9.

10. Fourth Lateran Council (1215) from *Enchiridion Symbolorum Definitinuem et Declarationium*, ed. Henry Denzinger and Adolf Schonmetzer, 33 ed. (Freiburg: Herder, 1965) in *Sacraments and Worship: The Sources of Christian Theology*. Johnson, Maxwell, ed. (Louisville: Westminster, 2012), 225-6, emphasis mine.

11. Schmemann, Alexander. *For the Life of the Word* (Crestwood: St. Vladimar's, 1976), 26, emphasis mine.

world immediately as the Body of Christ, So, we pray: "send us out to do the work you have given us to do, to love and serve you as faithful witnesses of Christ our Lord." [366] The deacon's dismissal asserts a relationship between the liturgy that we have participated in and the liturgy (or work) of our Christian life beyond the doors of the church.

> Together met, together bound,
> We'll go our different ways,
> And as [God's] people in the world
> We'll live and speak [God's] praise.[12]

When to use what prayers

Throughout this chapter, there has been references to many different Eucharistic prayers. Here's some general guidance when each prayer is particularly appropriate.

- Prayer A: Anytime
- Prayer B: Incarnational Cycle
- Prayer C: Ordinary Time, "Creation Season"
- Prayer D: Eastertide
- EOW 1: Paschal Cycle
- EOW 2: Incarnational, Ordinary Time, All Saints
- EOW 3: Day of Pentecost, Incarnational Cycle

Role of the Altar Guild

The sacristans of our Church play a vital role in the celebration of the Holy Eucharist. Sample checklists can be found in the appendices. However, the role is more than these necessary tasks. As sacristans, you can join with the clergy as holders of the theology and history

---

12. Wren, *Brian*. "I come with joy to meet my Lord." *The Hymnal 1982.* (New York: Church Hymnal, 1985), 304.

of the Eucharist. In this vocation, you can allow the liturgy's deep grammar to challenge and inspire the work you do, imbuing it with rich meaning, so that your ministry, in word and deed, can invite others into the sacredness and joy of the liturgy of the Church and our witness in the world.

God our Maker, whose Holy Child our Lord Jesus Christ in a wonderful Sacrament has left us a memorial of the Passion: Grant us so to venerate the sacred mysteries of Christ's Body and Blood, that we may ever perceive within ourselves the fruit of our redemption; who lives and reigns with you and the Holy Spirit, one God, for ever and ever. Amen. [252, modified]

CHAPTER TEN

HOLY BAPTISM AND CONFIRMATION

Jesus [said to the disciples], "All authority in heaven and on earth has been given to me. Go therefore and make disciples of all nations, baptizing them in the name of the Father and of the Son and of the Holy Spirit and teaching them to obey everything that I have commanded you."

(Matthew 28:18-19)

I am not a "cradle Episcopalian." At just a few weeks old, I was baptized by a Roman Catholic priest, who was a long-time family friend, in a private ceremony in the beautiful, gothic-styled chapel of the now-closed Queen of the Rosary Academy on Long Island. I was not a *practicing* member of the Roman Catholic Church for very long; my family joined the Episcopal Church before I entered the nursery school at the local parish, making me what I like to call a *baby carriage Episcopalian.*

"Will you be responsible for seeing the child you present is brought up in the Christian faith and life?" [302] This is the question asked of parents and godparents (or sponsors) when a young child is presented for baptism. While I obviously have no memory of my baptism, I do have many wonderful memories of being raised as a young Christian in the Church with the guidance and support of my parents, godparents, and members of the parish community. Sunday Eucharist, weekly Chapel Service at the parish school, Sunday School, and Bagel Hour (it was Long Island, after all)—these were all part of my formation as a Christian, along with the many people and clergy of the parish who cared for me and my nascent life of faith.

On a very warm day in June 1996, in the cathedral where a decade later I would take ordination vows, I *made* my confirmation. As the bishop reminded us during the sermon, this was not graduation from Sunday School but rather the commencement of the next stage of my life of faith begun in baptism: a journey of learning and spiritual development that continues to this day.

Holy Baptism

Baptism is the sacrament of initiation into the Christian faith and marks an individual's incorporation into the community of believers, the Church. The history of baptism in the Episcopal Church reflects a continuity with the broader Christian tradition, tracing its roots to the early Church and biblical accounts of baptism, including Jesus' own by John the Baptist in the Jordan River. Theologically, baptism is understood as a means of grace, a visible and effective sign of God's love and covenant with God's people. Our attention turns now to the development of the sacrament of Holy Baptism and the rite as it appears in the Book of Common Prayer.

The concept of ritual purification through water was well-established in Judaism, centuries before the emergence of Christianity. The Second Temple period Jewish purification rites or ritual water-baths, which developed into what today is called a *mikveh*, involved full immersion in water to achieve ritual cleanliness. This was done, particularly, in preparation for religious ceremonies, such as conversion, or after certain events that rendered one ritually impure.

> Now when all the people were baptized and when Jesus also had been baptized and was praying, the heaven was opened, and the Holy Spirit descended upon him in bodily form like a dove. And a voice came from heaven, "You are my Son, the Beloved; with you I am well pleased." (Luke 3:21-22)

John the Baptist can be seen as a bridge between Jewish purification rituals and Christian baptism. John's baptism was one of repentance and forgiveness of sins, carried out in the Jordan River. His call for repentance and his practice of baptism resonated with Jewish audiences familiar with the symbolic significance of water purification, yet it also introduced a new dimension that prepared the way for the messianic message of Jesus.

> As they were going along the road, they came to some water, and the eunuch said, "Look, here is water! What is to prevent me from being baptized?" He commanded the chariot to stop, and both of them, Philip and the eunuch, went down into the water, and Philip baptized him. (Acts 8:36-38)

For the first followers of Jesus, baptism became the rite of initiation into the community of believers. It was seen not only as a purification from sin but also as a rebirth and an entry into a new life in Christ. The *Acts of the Apostles* and the New Testament epistles provide early accounts of baptismal practices. Baptism was performed in the name of Jesus Christ, and not much later, in the name of the Father, the Son, and the Holy Spirit, as prescribed by the Great Commission (Matthew 28:19, see above).

> Those who are persuaded and believe that the things we teach and say are true, and promise that they can live accordingly… are brought by us where there is water, and are reborn by the same manner of rebirth by which we ourselves were reborn; for they are then washed in the water in the name of God the Father and Master of all, and of our Savior Jesus Christ, and of the Holy Spirit.[1]

> Justin Martyr (c. 155)

---

1. Justin Martyr. *First Apology*, LXI, LXV (c. 155), trans Edward Rochie Hardy in *Sacraments and Worship: The Sources of Christian Theology.* Johnson, Maxwell, ed. (Louisville: Westminster John Knox, 2012), 108.

Early Church teachers wrote often about the practices and theological significance of baptism. As a ritual practice, it not only cleansed one from unrighteousness and marked conversion but also conferred the same Holy Spirit that descended on Jesus to the newly baptized "at the time when they would become acquainted with Him."[2] Writing in the early 3rd century, Clement of the Alexandria noted the newly baptized would become the adopted children of God—an idea preserved in our prayer book: "you [God] have received us as your sons and daughters, made us citizens of your kingdom, and given us the Holy Spirit to guide us into all truth." [381]

In the early Church, baptisms was for adults and it often involved a period of catechesis, which lasted three years. The terms *catechesis* and *catechumen*, which is the term for the baptismal candidate, derive from the Greek word *katecheo*. The root *kata* means "thoroughly," and *echeo* means "to resound," and the method of instruction through repeated verbal teaching.

During this time, the catechumen would undergo instruction in Christian doctrine and moral teachings, engage in practices of prayer, fasting, and almsgiving, and would attend services of prayer, readings from Scripture, and instruction. They would not be permitted to participate in the celebration of the Holy Eucharist.

Though practice differs widely across the Episcopal Church, this remains the canonical teaching of the Church: the sharing of Holy Communion is for those who are baptized. Also, resources for local congregations that wish to restore the practice of the catechumenate, in a contemporary form, have been provided in the most recent revision of the *Book of Occasional Services*.

During Lent in their third year, catechumens would receive their final instruction in the Gospel and undergo a series of liturgical rites of exorcism and purification (later called *scrutinies*) to be prepared for baptism at the Great Vigil of Easter. Before their baptism,

---

2. *Ibid.*

catechumens would publicly renounce their former way of life and affirm their commitment to Christ and the Church.

In the ancient Church, the Great Vigil of Easter was the culmination of the catechumenate process. It was the most joyful celebration of the Christian year and its themes of light, life, and resurrection served as a powerful symbol of the Christian hope in the victory of Christ over sin and death. In a complex and richly symbolic ritual presided over by the bishop, catechumens were immersed three times in a pool of water, anointed abundantly with holy oils of exorcism and thanksgiving (today, catechumen and chrism, respectively), and marked with the sign of the cross. In the Old Testament, kings and priests were anointed; the earliest Christians understood baptismal anointing as sharing in the priesthood of all believers and in light of the first epistle of Peter: "You are a chosen race, a royal priesthood, a holy nation." (1 Pet 2:9) After anointing, the newly baptized donned a white robe and were welcomed by the faithful into the Church with the exchange of the peace and the celebration of the Holy Eucharist. (This could sound familiar to you as you think of our rites of baptism in today's Book of Common Prayer.)

By the late patristic period of the 4th to 6th centuries and following the declaration of Christianity as the official religion of the Roman Empire, "the loss of tension between the Church and the world, a lack of zeal on the part of many new converts, and the scarcity of clergy were to curtail the ritual."[3] It was during this time, as well, that there were theological conversations about original sin, infant baptism, and the rites of confirmation. We will discuss rites of confirmation shortly; however, it should be noted here that linking this rite with admittance to Holy Communion began in some places during this period and continued, in our tradition, until the 1979 revision of the Book of Common Prayer.

---

3. Hatchett, Marion. *Commentary on the American Prayer Book.* (New York: Harpers Collins, 1995), 255.

During the Middle Ages, the theology of baptism continued to emphasize its salvific and sacramental nature. However, there was an increased emphasis on the role of the Church hierarchy in administering the sacrament (i.e. christening a child or making one a Christian) and an increased diversity of prescribed rites and practices. Infant baptism became the norm, as the Church taught that baptism washed away original sin and secured the child's place in the Kingdom of Heaven. (It was only recently the Roman Catholic Church eliminated the concept of *limbo*, the place where the souls of unbaptized children would reside for eternity.) The practice of godparents, who would be responsible for ensuring the child's Christian upbringing along with the parents, became more formalized during this period both ecclesiastically and civilly.

> Baptism is the sign of the initiation by which we are received into the society of the Church, in order that, engrafted in Christ, we may be reckoned among God's children.[4]

> John Calvin (1559)

During the Reformation, the theology and practice of baptism underwent minor to significant changes as different Reformers sought to emphasize various aspects of the sacrament. Primarily, the rite was simplified and, in Protestant traditions, the anointing with oil was eliminated. The mode of baptism also varied, with some practicing immersion, while others practiced affusion (pouring) or aspersion (sprinkling).

Martin Luther and John Calvin affirmed the sacramental nature of baptism as a means of God's grace and affirmed the public celebration of baptism, including infant baptism. Both de-emphasized the role of ministers in performing the sacrament; it is God who acts through

---

4. Calvin, John. *Institutes of the Christian Religion* IV (1559) in *Sacraments and Worship: The Sources of Christian Theology.* Johnson, Maxwell, ed. (Louisville: Westminster John Knox, 2012), 160.

the rite, not the other way around. Menno Simons, who was the leader of the Anabaptist movement, argued against infant baptism since "young children are without understanding and unteachable."[5] This led to the idea of believers' (or adult) baptism, which continues to this day in various Christian traditions.

Today, the common practice in the Episcopal Church, and many mainline denominations, is to baptize infants, with parents and sponsors (godparents) taking vows on behalf of the child. However, with fewer parents opting to baptize young children, we could see more adult baptisms of adults as they convert to the Christian faith— what was old is new again, it is said.

> It appears by ancient writers, that the Sacrament of Baptism in the old time was not commonly ministered, but at two times in the year, at Easter and Whitsunday [Pentecost], at which times it was openly ministered in the presence of the congregation: Which custom (now being grown out of use) although it cannot for many considerations be well restored again, yet it is thought to good to follow the same as near as conveniently may be: Wherefore the people are to be admonished, that it is most convenient that baptism should not be ministered but upon Sundays and other holy days, when the most number of people can come together.[6]
>
> "Of the Administration of Public Baptism"
> in the Book of Common Prayer (1549)

Our attention turns now to the development of the rite of Holy Baptism in the 1979 edition of the Book of Common Prayer. Each edition of the prayer book offers unique insight into how the rite of

---

5. Simons, Menno. *Foundations of Christian Doctrine* (1539) in *Sacraments and Worship: The Sources of Christian Theology.* Johnson, Maxwell, ed. (Louisville: Westminster John Knox, 2012), 158.

6. "Of the Administration of Public Baptism" in *The First and Second Prayer Book of Edward VI* (New York: Dutton, 1952), 236. Spelling modernized.

baptism reflects the evolving liturgical and theological perspectives in the Anglican tradition.

In the 1549 edition of the Book of Common Prayer, Archbishop Cranmer revised a version of the medieval Sarum rite combined with the new German reformation texts. Baptisms were expected to be in public, though provisions were made for private baptisms and baptisms by laity in the case of emergency. It followed the Sarum custom of exhortation, naming, and exorcism at the entrance of the church before moving to the font. The three-fold immersion, vesting in white robe, and anointing with oil (chrismation) was also preserved, though the giving of a candle was eliminated.

The 1552 revision, also overseen by Cranmer, marked a significant shift towards a more reformed theology. The rite of Holy Baptism was to take place entirely at the font and exorcism, naming, and anointing with oil were omitted, though consignation (the making of the sign of the cross) was preserved. The three-fold renunciations and promises were reduced to one question. Private and emergency baptisms remained permitted. Though the Puritans wanted it eliminated altogether, the 1604 edition reworked the section on private baptism and made provision for baptism to be placed with Morning or Evening Prayer. Such a placement, in effect, made it that even public baptisms were largely attended by parents, godparents, and family only. Also, in this revision, lay people could no longer baptize in the event of an emergency; an ordained minister was needed.

The first American Book of Common Prayer (1789) retained much of the structure and language of the 1604 edition, unchanged in 1662. Slight revisions to the prayers and rubrics were made, including that parents could serve as sponsors, permission to remove consignation was given, and the recitation of the Apostles' Creed was replaced by a single question. Few changes were made until 1928, when consignation, the making of the sign of the cross on the forehead, was again required and permission for any Christian to baptize in the event of an emergency was restored within the rubrics. Chrismation was not permitted.

> We receive you into the household of God. Confess the faith of Christ crucified, proclaim [Christ's] resurrection, and share with us in [the] eternal priesthood. [308]

The Book of Common Prayer has presumed since 1549 that baptisms are public and part of the Sunday Eucharist. However, following common practice for centuries, "an author writing [in the Episcopal Church] in 1911 could rejoice that, due to the hard work of the last generations of clergy, baptisms were normally in private soon after the birth of the child."[7] Practices continue to vary from parish to parish: Most baptisms today, I dare say, are public celebrations on Sundays; some clergy will regularly offer private baptisms; some will make an exception for it; and, some will do private baptism in a pastoral emergency only.

Our attention turns now to the rite itself. We will look at the key components of the Presentation and Examination, Baptismal Covenant, Thanksgiving over the Water and Baptism, and Consignation and Chrismation.

Set within the context with the Holy Eucharist, the presider begins with the Opening Acclamation, as usual, with the addition of a dialogue between the priest and people based on Paul's admonition about unity to the Church in Ephesus: "there is one body and one Spirit, just as you were called to the *one hope of your calling*, one Lord, one faith, one baptism, *one God and Father of all*." (Ephesians 4:4-5, emphasis is mine)

Following the Sermon, the candidates for Baptism are presented by name by their sponsors. They are presented by name again at the Font; however, no provision is made for the presiding to say, "Name this child." The Church does not believe that one does not have a

---

7. Hatchett, 266.

name before they come to the waters of baptism. Adults and older children will answer the question "do you desire to be baptized?" while parents and godparents will speak on behalf of infants and young children. Parents and godparents promise to be responsible for seeing that the child they present is raised in the Christians faith and that by their prayers and witness they will help the child grow in Christ. [302]

The candidates, or the parents and godparents on their behalf, then make the three-fold renunciations and promises. Satan, a Hebrew word for "devil" or "adversary," is the personification of the forces of evil, wickedness, and sinful desires that rebel against God, corrupt those created by God, and draw humanity away from the love of God. [302] The renunciations connect the worldly and personal battles against evil with the cosmic one that we've seen played out throughout Scripture. The three-fold promises to follow and obey Jesus, putting trust in Christ's grace and love, balance out the renunciations. [302-3] It was ancient practice for the catechumens to physically turn and change the direction they were facing from West to East, the direction of the rising sun and new day. While this does not happen physically today, liturgical theologian Ruth Meyers reminds us "turning to Jesus Christ is an activity of heart, soul, mind. It is changing sides in a cosmic struggle."[8]

The next question asked by the presider is of great importance and connects to the ritual actions of the liturgy to the larger work of the Church, the liturgy outside of worship: "Will you who witness these vows do all in your power to support these persons in their life in Christ?" The prayer book reminds us that being a follower of Jesus is not individual endeavor but one that involves the prayer and support of the whole community. When young children are baptized and we answer "we will" to this question, are we considering what Christian formation looks like for them in our parishes? When older

---

8. Meyers, Ruth and Mitchell, Leonel. *Praying Shapes Believing: A Theological Commentary on the Book of Common Prayer.* (New York: Seabury, 2016), 115.

children and adults are baptized, are we considering what education in the faith looks like for them and what roles they will play in the community?

Together, in a sign of shared faith, the whole assembly recites the Apostles' Creed in a dialogue between the presider and people which is a restoration of ancient practices—and evidence that the creed emerged from the practice of baptism. In earlier editions of the Book of Common Prayer, there was a question asked if the candidate believed the Creeds—a further presumption that a credal statement of faith was made in the context of a Sunday Eucharist. The Baptismal Covenant combines the credal statements with the beliefs of how the Christian faith and life is lived: continuing in the apostles' teaching, sharing in Communion, resisting sin and evil and seeking forgiveness, proclaiming the Good News, loving our neighbor as ourselves, and striving for justice and peace. [304-5]

The presider bids prayers for the candidates that they may fulfill what they have promised. The intercessions may be offered by a member of the congregation or by one of the sponsors [see 312]. The concluding collect "brings out not only the symbolism of death and resurrection in baptism but also the eschatological implications of the rite."[9]

The Thanksgiving over the Water that follows reflects what we believe about God's actions throughout salvation history, as well as what we believe about the sacrament of baptism itself. A fulsome prayer that restores Old Testament imagery, it alludes to the Spirit moving over the waters of creation (Genesis 1:2) and passing through the waters of the Red Sea from slavery to freedom (Exodus 14:22). It turns to Jesus receiving the baptism of John in the waters of the Jordan River (Mark 1:9-11) and then profoundly to our connection to Jesus' life, death, and resurrection. Meyers notes, "the prayer sets forth participation in Christ's death and resurrection, new birth in the

---

9. Hatchett, 274.

Holy Spirit, and commissioning to preach the Good News to world as the effects of the sacrament."[10]

The ritual water-bath follows immediately. The prayer book still assumes full immersion, but very few parishes in the Episcopal Church practice that. Water is poured over the candidate using the baptismal formula based on Matthew 28:19: "Go therefore and make disciples of all nations, baptizing them *in the name of the Father and of the Son and of the Holy Spirit*" (emphasis is mine).

The giving of a baptismal candle, lit from the Paschal Candle, may take place here. Then follows the prayer for the gifts of the Spirit, which in previous editions had appeared in the rites for Confirmation. This makes clear the prayer book's teaching that baptism is full initiation into the life of the Church. [298]

Consignation, along with the anointing with oil (chrismation) if desired, is then done. The prayer book directs that the bishop, or priest, places a hand on each person's head, making the sign of the cross on the forehead, saying: "You are sealed by the Holy Spirit and Baptism and marked as Christ's own forever." [308] The optional use of chrism here reintroduces the ancient early Church practice of anointing with oil, abundantly hopefully, after baptism.

The newly baptized are then ritually welcomed into the congregation and the larger Body of Christ. This is done first through the spoken response of the congregation to the baptism receiving them into the household of God [308], then the Exchange of the Peace among all present, and finally in the sharing of the Holy Eucharist.

The Book of Common Prayer recommends that the following Sundays are particularly appropriate for baptism: First Sunday after the Epiphany: Baptism of Our Lord; Great Vigil of Easter; Day of Pentecost; All Saints' Sunday; and when the bishop visits. Some congregations adhere to this practice solely, others do not, and many practice something in between. It is important that the Altar Guild

---

10. Meyers, 120.

know the practices of the clergy and the traditional practices of your congregation.

The Altar Guild's responsibilities for preparing for the rite of Holy Baptism will inevitably include various tasks. Sample checklists have been provided in the appendix, along with those for the other initiation rites.

> Heavenly Father, we thank you that by water and the Holy Spirit you have bestowed upon these your servants the forgiveness of sin, and have raised them to the new life of grace. Sustain them, O Lord, in your Holy Spirit. Give them an inquiring and discerning heart, the courage to will and to persevere, a spirit to know and to love you, and the gift of joy and wonder in all your works. Amen. [308]

Confirmation and Other Rites

One day while walking out of liturgics class while in seminary, a classmate turned to a group of us and said wryly: "Confirmation really is a theological tease." He wasn't wrong. Often referred to as a sacrament in search of a theology, Confirmation, as a rite, has taken many forms over the centuries. This sacrament's development is intertwined with the history of Christian initiation rites, theological interpretations, and liturgical practices. One of the seven sacramental rites of the Church, it marks a deepening of God's grace and the strengthening of the individual's bond with the Church in the form of an adult affirmation of baptismal faith.

In the earliest days of Christianity, the rites of baptism, confirmation, and Eucharist were often performed together as a unified process of initiation, typically during the Great Easter Vigil. The Acts of the Apostles does record the laying on of hands and the receiving of the Holy Spirit as distinct yet closely associated with baptism. In Acts 8:14-17, the apostles Peter and John lay hands on baptized Samaritans to confer the Holy Spirit; though, that was to those who were only baptized in the name of Jesus.

By the 4th century, the rites of baptism and confirmation began to separate, particularly in the Western Church. This divergence was largely due to the increasing number of converts and the logistical difficulties for bishops, who were traditionally the ones to perform the rite of initiation, to be present at every baptism. In some places, the priest would do the water-bath and then the bishop, separately, anoints with chrism. However, even in the 6th century, Pope Gregory I still calls for the unity of the rite, allowing priests to anoint with chrism, which has been blessed by the bishop, when a bishop could not be present.

By the thirteenth century, confirmation had evolved to become a sacrament in and of itself. Thomas Aquinas noted that "it is clear that confirmation is a special sacrament" by which the mature Christian grows in baptismal grace and strengthening.[11] The late 15th century Council of Florence moved the chrismation of baptism to the rite of confirmation, marking it as the completion of the rite of initiation and the conferring of the Holy Spirit. This remained the theological understanding of the Catholic Church until the Second Vatican Council (1962-65).

Not known for his subtle opposition, Calvin led the opposition to the rite of confirmation as a separate sacrament during the Protestant Reformation. He wrote:

> I hasten to declare that I am certainly not of the number of those who think that confirmation, as observed under the Roman papacy, is an idle ceremony, inasmuch as I regard it as one of the most deadly wiles of Satan. Let us remember that this pretended sacrament is nowhere recommended in Scripture. ... And with this they joined detestable blasphemy, because they said that sins were only forgiven by baptism,

---

11. Thomas Aquinas, "Confirmation," in *Summa Theologiae*, Q.72, art 1, Reply, in *Sacraments and Worship: The Sources of Christian Theology*. Johnson, Maxwell, ed. (Louisville: Westminster John Knox, 2012), 156.

and that the Spirit of regeneration is given by that rotten oil which they presumed to bring in without the word of God.[12]

Anglicanism, as usual in finding its way in the middle of contrasting ideas, never viewed confirmation as harshly and maintained both ancient and reformed practices. Confirmation has not been seen as the moment of spiritual regeneration or rebirth (that is baptism); though, confirmation has been mainly tied to the reception of Holy Communion. After baptism, infants, children, and converts would receive instruction in the faith (in ancient days called *mystogogy*) and, upon examination and confirmation by the bishop, they would then be admitted to Communion. In order to better understand the rite in Anglicanism today, our attention turns to theological and liturgical shifts from 1549 to 1979.

The 1549 Book of Common Prayer retained many elements of the medieval English Church. The primary purpose of confirmation in this edition was to ensure those who had been baptized as infants were examined in their faith and marked with the sign of the cross (not anointed, as that happened in baptism). While separate, it was a complementary rite to baptism, intended to confirm and strengthen the faith of those already baptized. In 1552, consignation was moved from the confirmation rite to baptism and the baptismal anointing, as noted earlier, was eliminated. Confirmation remained Cranmer's prayer written for edition remains, with slight edits, even in today's prayer book:

Defend, O Lord, this child with thy heavenly grace, that he may continue thine for ever and daily increase in thy holy spirit more and more, until he comes unto thy everlasting kingdom. Amen.[13]

12. Calvin, John, "Confirmation" in *Tracts containing Antidote to the Council of Trent* in in *Sacraments and Worship: The Sources of Christian Theology*. Johnson, Maxwell, ed. (Louisville: Westminster John Knox, 2012), 161.

13. "Of Confirmation," *The First and Second Prayer Book of Edward VI* (New York: Dutton, 1952), 408. Spelling modernized.

This first prayer book of the Episcopal Church (1789) maintained the importance of the bishop's role in Confirmation, as well as the importance of catechetical preparation. Through the 1928 edition, it remained the sacrament by which one entered Holy Communion.

The 1979 edition of the Book of Common Prayer marks a significant departure from previous editions, incorporating insights from the liturgical renewal movement and the Second Vatican Council. The confirmation rite in this edition highlights the strengthening of the gifts of the Holy Spirit given in baptism and the confirmand's continued role in the mission and ministry of the Church. It also removes the connection between Confirmation and participation in the Holy Eucharist; though, it makes no distinct provision for when one could share in receiving Holy Communion. For infants and young children, the common practice seems to be at the discretion of the parents. Today, the sacramental rite of Confirmation is an affirmation of faith by an adult and a liturgical "act by which a baptized person personally accepts the faith into which he or she has been baptized and renews the promise to live the baptismal life."[14]

The "age of maturity," as it is sometimes called, often varies from diocese to diocese and even congregation to congregation. The bishop, as the chief pastor in the diocese, or another bishop assigned, is the confirming minister, emphasizing the sacrament's connection to the broader Church and its apostolic traditions. The rite of confirmation includes the renewal of baptismal vows and the laying on of hands and prayer over the candidate by the bishop. In some cases, the anointing with chrism still takes place, though the theological reasoning for that in this rite remains nebulous, at best.

In the end, Confirmation remains a sacrament in search of a significant theology. It is clear it is not a rite of passage from adolescence to adulthood; as a liturgical act, it needs to be more meaningful. Some may see it as a confirmation of the baptism rather than the person,

---

14. Meyers, 138.

though that lacks some merit. Meyers may describe the preservation of the rite of confirmation best when she says: "it is more reasonable to assume that the General Convention simply wished to maintain the practice to which the Church was accustomed."[15]

The prayer book also provides for two other rites around Christian initiation: Reaffirmation and Reception. Reaffirmation gives a confirmed Christian the opportunity to public reaffirm their baptismal faith in the presence of the bishop. This is often done when someone has been separated from the Church for some time and wishes to acknowledge their return to the fold. It can also be done by someone during a major life change or when taking on a new ministry in the life of the Church. Reception is when someone baptized and confirmed in another tradition is welcomed officially into the Episcopal Church and the larger Anglican Communion. The role of the bishop, as chief pastor of the diocese, remains an important symbol in both ritual acts.

As it has for millennia, the Church will continue to reflect on our theology and practice. For now, the theology and rites of Holy Baptism, Confirmation, Reaffirmation, and Reception in the Book of Common Prayer reflect the Episcopal Church's commitment to, and best understanding of, sacramental living, spiritual formation, and communal life and worship.

All praise and thanks to you, most merciful Father, for adopting us as your own children, for incorporating us into your holy Church, and for making us worthy to share in the inheritance of the saints in light; through Jesus Christ your Son our Lord, who lives and reigns with you and the Holy Spirit, one God, for ever and ever. Amen. [311]

---

15. Ibid, 139.

CHAPTER ELEVEN

THE DAILY OFFICES

*A hallmark of the Anglican tradition is the prayer of the daily office.
The genius of Thomas Cranmer was the simplification of the medieval
office, which had grown to be a very complex and confusing round of
daily prayer largely the prerogative of monks and clergy. Cranmer's
solution was to create an office accessible to the people of God and
for their edification.*

Jean Campbell[1]

"Glorify the Lord, O chill and cold, drops of dew and flakes of snow. Frost and cold, ice and sleet, glorify the Lord," [88] took on new meaning as we traipsed from the rectory through the freshly fallen snow to pray Morning Prayer in the beautiful and chilly stone church. "Now as we come to the setting of the sun, and our eyes behold the vesper light, we sing thy praises, O God: Father, Son, and Holy Spirit," [64] was enhanced as we looked out from *The Crags*, a home belonging to parishioners, and saw the light of the so-called golden hour reflecting off blue-green waters of the Gulf of Maine.

It is nearly impossible for me to think about the Daily Offices without remembering James, my mentor priest and a dear friend. At the time of his death in 2010, he was serving as rector of a parish in Maine. Visits over the years always included saying the Offices together, as he prayed them daily and encouraged his parish to join him regularly.

A cornerstone of the communal worship of the Episcopal Church, this structured cycle of prayer encompasses Morning and Evening Prayer, as well as lesser offices of Noonday Prayer and Compline. It

---

1. Campbell, Jean, OSH. "The Daily Prayer of the Church." *A Prayer Book for the 21st Century: Liturgical Studies 3*. (New York: Church Pension Fund, 1996), 2.

provides a space for prayer and reflection that grounds our day-to-day living in the Church Calendar, the Psalms, and Scripture. Rooted in ancient traditions, the Daily Offices also exemplify the Episcopal Church's commitment to a rich and disciplined spiritual life as an extension of the Sunday morning Eucharist.

As we begin this exploration into the history, theology, and structure of the Daily Offices, it's good to start with a definition. The word *office* has its origins in the Latin word *officium*, which means "service," "duty," or "ceremony." Derived from *opus*, meaning "work," and *facere*, meaning "to do," *officium* broadly denotes a task or duty that one is obliged to perform. The etymology of *office* in Christian prayer practice underscores the notion of prayer as a devoted, structured service to God, integral to the daily rhythm of a religious life.

> I will call upon God, and the Lord will deliver me. In the evening, in the morning, and at noonday, I will complain and lament, and [God] will hear my voice. (Psalm 55:17-18)

The roots of the Daily Offices can be traced back to the prayer practices of ancient Judaism. Jewish tradition prescribed specific times for prayer, with roots in the Torah and further elaborated in rabbinic literature.

The first Christians simply continued this practice as they knew it. The Acts of the Apostles (4:23–30) tells us that Jewish-Christians prayed the Psalms daily and this has remained a principal part of the offices down through the millennia. By 60 CE, the *Didache*, recommends disciples to pray the Lord's Prayer three times a day. This practice found its way into the Daily Offices, as well.

> Prayer is, then, to speak more boldly, converse with God.
>
> Clement of Alexandria[2]

---

2. Clement of Alexandria, *Stromata or Miscellanies*, VII, 7 (ca 200), trans William Wilson in *Sacraments and Worship: The Sources of Christian Theology*. Johnson, Maxwell, ed. (Louisville: Westminster John Knox, 2012), 346.

By the second century, Clement of Alexandria, Origen, and Tertullian all wrote of the practice of Morning and Evening Prayer, and of the prayers at the third, sixth, and ninth hours. Christian monasticism, beginning around the 3rd century with figures like Anthony of Egypt and Syncletica of Alexandria, called the Desert Fathers and Mothers, played a crucial role in developing structured daily prayer.

> The Prophet says: "Seven times a day have I praised you." We will fulfill this sacred number of seven if we satisfy our obligations of service…The same prophet says, "At midnight I arose to give you praise."
>
> From the *Rule of St. Benedict*[3]

Using desert monasticism as inspiration, later monastic communities sought to organize their lives around regular intervals of prayer and work (*ora et labora*). The Divine Office, also known as the Liturgy of the Hours, became the formal structure of daily prayer in monastic communities. St. Benedict's Rule, written in the 6th century, prescribed a schedule of eight daily offices: Matins (around 2:00am), Lauds (early morning), Prime (at first day light), Terce (around 9:00am), Sext (Noon), None (ninth hour, around 3pm), Vespers (around sunset), and Compline (before sleep). These offices were primarily composed of Psalms, hymns, readings, and prayers, and this structure deeply influenced the development of the Daily Offices in the wider Christian tradition, and possibly even beyond.

Let's take a step outside Christianity for a moment. Structured daily prayer is not limited to our Judeo-Christian tradition. For example, Islam, emerging in the 7th century, also formalized a system of daily prayers known as *Salah*. Muslims are required to pray five times a day at prescribed times: Fajr (dawn), Dhuhr (midday), Asr

---

3. Fry, Timothy, ed. *The Rule of St. Benedict in English.* (Collegeville: The Liturgical Press, 1982), 44.

(afternoon), Maghrib (sunset), and Isha (night). Any student of religious, and even secular, traditions, would be hard-pressed to find one that did not promote daily reflection and meditation.

> A cleric, inasmuch as he is a cleric and especially as he has been established in sacred orders, is required to say the canonical hours. Indeed, it seems that such persons have been claimed for divine praise, as it says in Isaiah 43: "Everyone who is called by my name, for my praise I created them;" and inasmuch as the cleric is a beneficiary in this church, he is required to say the office according to the way of the church.
>
> Thomas Aquinas[4]

In Christianity, during the later Medieval period the Liturgy of the Hours developed into the structured and integral component of monastic and larger ecclesiastical life that we recognize today, in some form. Each of these hours included specific psalms, hymns, readings, and prayers. The content varied depending on the time of day, the liturgical season, and whether it was a feast day or an ordinary day.

Matins included a series of psalms, readings from Scripture, and writings of the Church Fathers. *Lauds and Vespers*, known as the principal hours, included a significant number of psalms, a hymn, a Scripture reading, the Canticle of Zechariah (*Benedictus*) at Lauds, and the Canticle of Mary (*Magnificat*) at Vespers. *Prime, Terce, Sext,* and *None*, known as the "little hours," were shorter offices focused on psalms, a hymn, and a brief Scripture reading. The final office of the day, *Compline*, included an examination of conscience, psalms, the Canticle of Simeon (*Nunc Dimittis*), and prayers for a peaceful night.

---

4. Thomas Aquinas. *Quaestiones quodlibetales* III, q. 13, a 2. in *Sacraments and Worship: The Sources of Christian Theology.* Johnson, Maxwell, ed. (Louisville: Westminster John Knox, 2012), 361.

While the full Liturgy of the Hours was primarily observed in monastic communities, cathedral clergy also followed a version of these prayers and parish clergy often had modified and shorter versions due to their pastoral duties. For the laity, participation in the Liturgy of the Hours varied.

The prescribed orders for the Liturgy of the Hours, sometimes called the canonical hours, expanded continually. By the late Medieval period, there were five principal books that served as framework for these offices. The book of Psalms, called the *Psalter*, formed the backbone for these services. The *Lectionary* held the readings from Scripture and the Church Fathers. The *Antiphonary* contained the antiphons and responsories chanted and the *Hymnal* collected hymns sung during these times of worship. The *Breviary* was the book with the assigned orders and prayers for these canonical hours.

The structure of the Liturgy of the Hours and the specific texts used could vary significantly between different monastic orders and regions. For example, the Cistercians, Carthusians, and later the Franciscans followed simpler forms of the Office compared to the elaborate practices of Cluniac monasteries.

Throughout the Middle Ages, various attempts were made to standardize the Liturgy of the Hours. The Carolingian reforms in the 8th and 9th centuries, led by figures such as Charlemagne and Alcuin of York, aimed to unify liturgical practices across the Frankish Empire. The Fourth Lateran Council in 1215, and subsequent papal directives, further emphasized uniformity in liturgical practice.

In monastic communities, the Liturgy of the Hours dictated the rhythm of the day, structuring the monks' time around prayer, work, and study. The recitation of the Divine Office also played a role in education, particularly within monastic and cathedral schools and universities. In broader society, the public celebration of the canonical hours in cathedrals and larger parish churches marked the passage of time. Bells ringing throughout the day for these liturgies regulated the daily life of towns and villages, calling people to prayer and reflection—or more accurately, letting them know that the clergy and monastics were praying in their churches.

> All priests and deacons shall be bound to say daily Morning and Evening Prayer, either privately or openly, except when letted [prevented] by preaching, studying of divinity, or by some other urgent cause. And the curate that ministers in every parish church or chapel, being at home, and not being otherwise reasonably letted, shall say the same in the parish church or chapel where he ministers, and shall toll a bell thereto, a convenient time before he begins, that such as be disposed may come to hear God's word, and to pray with him.
>
> "The Preface" to the Book of Common Prayer (1552)[5]

By the time of English Reformation in the 16th century, the offices within cathedrals had become "reasonably brief, colorful, ceremonious, odiferous, and full of movement... very churchy, somewhat vulgar, clergy-dominated, and impossibly simple to participate in."[6] The reformers in the Church of England, led by Archbishop Thomas Cranmer, sought to revive some ancient monastic and ascetical practices, simplify the practice of liturgy, and provide for the edification of the faithful.

The first Book of Common Prayer (1549) significantly reformed the Liturgy of the Hours. Cranmer condensed the eight monastic offices into two: Morning Prayer (Matins) and Evening Prayer (Evensong). Also, as we see from the Preface to the 1552 revision, this simplification aimed to encourage greater lay participation in the praying of the daily offices. This practice of daily prayer, with the

---

5. "The Preface," *The First and Second Prayer Book of Edward VI* (New York: Dutton, 1952), 323. Spelling modernized.

6. Meyers, Ruth and Mitchell, Leonel. *Praying Shapes Believing: A Theological Commentary on the Book of Common Prayer.* (New York: Seabury, 2016), 38.

tolling of the bell before, continues in many parishes of the Church of England to this day.

The 1662 edition of the Book of Common Prayer, which remains a cornerstone of Anglican liturgy, further solidified the structure of the Daily Offices. Morning and Evening Prayer in this edition provided a more robust framework of the Psalms, Scripture readings, canticles, and prayers, again accessible to both clergy and laity. This framework was preserved in the first American prayer books, as well.

We have seen the influence of the liturgical renewal movement of the late 19th and 20th centuries and how both sought to recover ancient practices and make liturgy more relevant to contemporary worshippers. That said, even in the 1979 revision of the prayer book, "except for linguistic changes and the addition of prayers, the structure and texts of Morning and Evening Prayer have remained constant in every Book of Common Prayer since 1549."[7]

> If the heart of the [1979] prayer book is the celebration of the paschal mystery of Christ in baptism and eucharist, then its soul may be the daily office.
>
> Jeffrey Lee[8]

This edition of the Book of Common Prayer continues the tradition of Morning and Evening Prayer with both orders for Rite One and Rite Two. Rite One provides for traditional language and Rite Two offers contemporary language. Both provide a greater variety of canticles, collects, and prayers and allow for more adaptation to different church seasons. In addition to Morning and Evening Prayers, the prayer book reintroduces other lesser offices: Noonday Prayer and Compline. Noonday Prayer provides a brief, focused opportunity for midday reflection and renewal. Compline, the final office of the day,

---

7. Campbell, 2.

8. Lee, Jefferey. *Opening the Prayer Book.* The New Church's Teaching Series: Volume Seven. (Cambridge: Cowley Publications, 1999), 114.

offers a more contemplative and peaceful conclusion to the day's prayers.

Enriching our Worship 1, published in 1997, offers an expansive approach to the traditional Daily Offices. The Standing Commission on Liturgy and Music incorporated inclusive language that seeks to broaden the imagery and metaphors used for God. New and revised invitatory psalms along with Scriptural and non-biblical canticles have been included, as well.

Our attention turns now to a brief overview of these offices. We will see that the Daily Offices embody several key themes: a discipline of prayer, immersion in psalms and lessons from Scripture, community and continuity of tradition, and the incarnational presence of God in our daily lives.

Morning Prayer

> Send out your light and your truth, that they may lead me, and
> bring me to your holy hill and to your dwelling. (Psalm 43:3)

Morning Prayer consists of several key components: the Opening Sentences, Confession of Sin, Invitatory and Psalter, Readings, Canticles, the Apostles' Creed, Prayers, and a Concluding Rite. The service begins with one or more sentences of Scripture appropriate to the season or occasion, such as the one above from the Psalms. After the opening sentences, a confession of sin may be offered, acknowledging our turning from the ways of God and our seeking of God's mercy.

The Invitatory Psalm and the appointed psalm(s) for the day then follow. The Invitatory Psalm serves as an invitation to worship and is often accompanied by an antiphon, which is a refrain that highlights a particular theme. The Psalter is central to the Daily Office, reflecting the ancient practice of reciting the psalms regularly. The psalms provide a rich tapestry of prayer, encompassing praise, lament, thanksgiving, and supplication. The assigned readings from Scripture follow the Psalms.

The Psalms and lessons are found in the Daily Office Lectionary in the prayer book (page 934 and following). Detailed instructions are given as to how to use the lectionary, as it can be complicated to understand at first. Unlike the Eucharistic lectionary, the Daily Office Lectionary is divided into a two-year cycle, aptly called Year One and Year Two.

After each reading, a canticle is sung or recited. Canticles provide a lyrical and meditative response to the readings, linking the hymns of the Old and New Testaments with the worshipping community's voice. These biblical songs or hymns of praise include among others: The Song of Zechariah (Luke 1:68-79), the First Song of Isaiah (Isaiah 12:2-6), The Song of the Redeemed (Rev 15:3-4), A Song of Creation (Song of Three Young Men, 35-65) and, the ancient hymn, *Te Deum laudamus*. A full listing and suggested usage is found on pages 144-145 and on pages 44-45 in *Enriching our Worship 1*.

The Apostles' Creed is then recited. This ancient creed unites the worshippers with the historical and global Church, grounding the liturgy in the shared tenets of Christianity.

The prayer section begins with the Lord's Prayer, a foundational prayer given by Jesus and from which all our prayer flows. Following this, a series of suffrages—or responsive petitions—are offered, leading into the Collects. The Collects include the one for the day, which corresponds to the liturgical calendar, and additional prayers for peace, grace, and other specific intentions. This section often includes space for intercessions and thanksgivings, allowing the congregation to pray for personal, communal, and worldly concerns.

While a sermon may be offered, it is not required. An office hymn or anthem by the choir, if present, may also be sung. Morning Prayer concludes with a General Thanksgiving and/or a Prayer of St. Chrysostom, the *benedicamus* ("Let us bless the Lord") and a sentence of scripture.

In corporate settings, Morning Prayer can be a standalone service or integrated into other liturgical practices, such as the Eucharist. It may be led by clergy or lay people, following the rubrics of the rite. For individuals, Morning Prayer offers a structured yet adaptable framework for daily devotions and meditation.

Evening Prayer

> Let my prayer be set forth in your sight as incense, the lifting
> up of my hands as the evening sacrifice. (Psalm 141:2)

Evening Prayer mirrors the structure of Morning Prayer. The invitatory hymn, *Phos hilaron* ("O gracious light"), dates to the 4th century liturgy of St. Basil the Great and is associated with the lighting of lamps and candles for the evening and night hours.

The Daily Office lectionary anticipates the reading of one lesson, though two or three may be read. The evening canticles of the *Magnificat* (Song of Mary) and the *Nunc Dimittis* (Song of Simeon) are sung or said, although again other canticles may be used (see BCP p. 145). Two sets of suffrages are provided: A is the same as Morning Prayer, while B is based on the Byzantine evening liturgy and echoes the themes of Evening Prayer: pardon, peace, and protection through the night.

Choral Evensong

Over the last quarter century, most notably in England, a trend has emerged: a growing number of people interested in Choral Evensong and its distinctive musical character. In the Episcopal Church, many of our cathedrals and larger parishes, especially those with strong music programs, offer Choral Evensong with regularity. Increasingly, even churches not of our denomination have discovered the appeal of this style of worship, rooted in monasticism.

Evensong is the name given to the sung version of Evening Prayer beginning with the first edition of the Book of Common

Prayer in 1549. Our prayer book and hymnal provide for this in both congregational and choral settings.

Choral Evensong is the practice of a choir and clergy singing most of the service—psalms, canticles, suffrages, collects—allowing the worshipper to participate by listening, with their ears and their heart, and allowing the words and prayers of the liturgy to wash over and surround them. The Reverend Simon Reynolds, former Canon Succentor of St. Paul's Cathedral in London (UK), describes Choral Evensong this way:

> Evensong is an act of worship that invites rather than compels. It allows us to gradually feel at home in its centuries-old contours, and to bring to it our own deeply felt needs and persistent hopes. It also allows us to catch the echoes and resonances of God speaking through the beauty of what our senses receive: to be comforted and challenged by the words and music; and to be encouraged to respond without specifying what that response must be. Our freedom to simply *be* is one of the outcomes of the choir, clergy, and others leading the worship by using their gifts and skills, often after many years of disciplined study and practice, to carry our hopes, our burdens, and our prayers.[9]

Order for Evening Worship

All the people congregate once more in the Anastasis, and the lamps and candles are lit, which makes it very bright. ... For some time they have the Lucernare psalms.

From the *Pilgrimage of Egeria (c. 384)*[10]

---

9. Reynolds, Simon. *Lighten our Darkness: Discovering and celebrating Choral Evensong.* (London: Darton, Longman, and Todd, 2021), 25.

10. Egeria, *Pilgrimage of Egeria,* XXIV-XXV (ca 384), trans. John Wilkinson, in *Egeria's Travels* (London: SPCK, 1971) in *Sacraments and Worship: The Sources of Christian Theology.* Johnson, Maxwell, ed. (Louisville: Westminster John Knox, 2012) 354.

The Order of Evening Worship is a more flexible order for Evening Prayer with a significant focus placed on the *lucerinarium* or lighting of the candles. An infrequently used order for liturgy, "it is particularly useful for the congregation which does not gather regularly for Evening Prayer but wishes to sing Evensong with some dignity and ceremony on a particular occasion."[11]

The liturgy begins with the traditional hymn in praise of light and the candle-lighting follows, which has its roots in ancient Ambrosian vesper rites and, as we see above, in the 4th century rites in Jerusalem. The *Book of Occasional Services* provides additional resources for this rite. The flexibility of this rite allows it to be used as a gathering rite during Evening Prayer or for the Eucharist. It may also be used as standalone liturgy with the addition of lessons from Scripture, psalm, canticles, and prayers at the discretion of the officiant, allowing for creativity and flexibility in liturgical planning.

Noonday Prayer

> Almighty Savior, who at noonday called your servant Saint Paul to be an apostle to the Gentiles: We pray you to illumine the world with the radiance of your glory, that all nations may come and worship you; for you live and reign for ever and ever. Amen. [107]

A modern adaptation of the monastic office of Sext, Noonday Prayer is one of the two lesser offices in the prayer book. It includes an opening sentence, psalms, a short passage of scripture, the Lord's Prayer, and collects. While the prayer book neither requires nor expects its use, it is included in the 1979 revision as a resource for communal worship when deemed appropriate, such as for retreats,

---

11. Meyers, Ruth and Mitchell, Leonel. *Praying Shapes Believing: A Theological Commentary on the Book of Common Prayer.* (New York: Seabury, 2016), 66.

diocesan conventions, or the like. During the COVID-19 pandemic separation from our houses of worship, many of our parishes adopted the practice of daily online Noonday Prayer to keep our congregations connected through prayer. It may also be used as a personal spiritual devotion and practice.

Compline

> The Lord Almighty grant us a peaceful night and a perfect rest. [127]

Compline is the other lesser office in the prayer book. A contemplative service designed for the end of the day, it is traditionally prayed before retiring for the night. Historically, the "great silence" began in monastic communities at the conclusion of Compline, when not a word was spoken until Matins—with the praise of God upon waking.

In practice in most of our congregations, it is often held at the conclusion of evening meetings or gatherings. Some congregations—such as St. Mark's Cathedral in Seattle, Washington, and Christ Church in Rochester, New York—have developed very well-attended public services of Compline. Like Choral Evensong, this monastic service attracts worshippers who wish to connect to ancient tradition in a constantly evolving world.

The order itself begins with an opening sentence and a confession of sin, allowing worshippers to seek God's forgiveness and peace. The psalms and Scriptural readings, typically short and focused on trust and safety, are read. Prayers and collects that follow include petitions for a peaceful night and protection from harm in the coming night. The service concludes with the canticle *Nunc Dimittis* (the Song of Simeon) with the antiphon: "Guide us waking, O Lord, and guard us sleeping; that awake we may watch with Christ and asleep we may rest in peace." [134]

Altar Guild and the Offices

While the primary focus of the Altar Guild is often associated with preparation for Eucharistic services, its role extends to the broader worship life of the Church, including the Daily Offices. The Altar Guild can contribute to worship in the Daily Offices through a variety of responsibilities:

1. *Set-Up and Arrangement*: Altar Guild members prepare the worship space for daily offices by arranging liturgical elements such as candles and incense. Depending on the liturgical season or feast, Altar Guild members might coordinate the use of appropriate liturgical colors and paraments.

2. *Liturgical Books and Materials:* The Altar Guild ensures that liturgical books, such as the Book of Common Prayer, bibles, hymnals, and any other materials needed for the Daily Office, are arranged and accessible to clergy, officiant, and participants.

3. *Special Occasions and Seasons:* For special occasions or seasons, such as Advent or Lent, the Altar Guild might need to adjust the setup to reflect the particular themes and liturgical practices associated with these times.

4. *Coordination with Clergy and Worship Leaders:* Altar Guild members should work closely with clergy and worship leaders to understand any specific liturgical preferences or variations for the Daily Office.

Conclusion

A rich inheritance from ancient Jewish practices, Christian monasticism, medieval liturgical traditions, and the English Reformation, the Daily Offices in the Book of Common Prayer offer a comprehensive, and at times flexible, framework for routine prayer that connects practitioners to the ancient rhythms of daily prayer and beyond themselves to the universal Church in worship. The Daily Offices seek to nurture a deep and sustained spiritual life, extending from our Sunday Eucharist and grounding us in the abiding presence of God throughout the day.

Almighty God, who hast promised to hear the petitions of those who ask in thy Son's Name: We beseech thee mercifully to incline thine ear to us who have now made our prayers and supplications unto thee; and grant that those things which we have faithfully asked according to thy will, may effectually be obtained, to the relief of our necessity, and to the setting forth of thy glory; through Jesus Christ our Lord. Amen. [834]

CHAPTER TWELVE

PASTORAL OFFICES

The Eucharist, the Daily Offices, and Christian initiation are integrated into the celebration of the liturgical year. The pastoral offices, on the other hand, are geared to the pattern of individual life.[1]

Ruth Meyers

Hurricane Irene was headed for Long Island and would make landfall just after midnight. It was late August, and it was hot and extremely humid. The cathedral didn't have air-conditioning and there was scaffolding up in half of the cathedral nave so trying to get any meaningful air-flow was very difficult. The bridal party had made their way in, followed by the flower girl and ring-bearer; the groomsmen were waiting with the celebrant; the organist was vamping. But where was the bride?

There was a flurry of activity in the narthex, and finally the doors opened as the *en chamade* pipes sounded the fanfare. As she had wanted, the bride began the entrance down the center aisle by herself, only to stop and then begin again. When she stopped the second time, midway, the groom rushed to join her, and together they walked the rest of way. With a smile and a few deep breaths, we were ready to start.

Later the organist and I learned that she had been overcome with all sorts of emotion. She needed words of encouragement, and the only people around were the wedding verger and a few other members of the Altar Guild. Reassured by their love and support, the bride took a deep breath and made her journey down the aisle.

---

1. Meyers, Ruth and Mitchell, Leonel. *Praying Shapes Believing: A Theological Commentary on the Book of Common Prayer.* (New York: Seabury, 2016), 213.

Our attention turns now to the pastoral liturgies of the Book of Common Prayer. Weddings, funerals, healing services, and other liturgies are filled with meaningful symbolism and often involve more detailed and careful work on the part of the Altar Guild. It is also in these liturgies where members of the Altar Guild, sacristans, and vergers are called upon to share in the ministry of pastoral care. Often this ministry requires a good bit of encouragement and love on top of remembering all the details.

Celebration and Blessing of a Marriage

> Set me as a seal upon your heart, as a seal upon your arm; for love is strong as death, passion fierce as the grave. Its flashes are flashes of fire, a raging flame. Many waters cannot quench love, neither can floods drown it.
>
> Song of Songs 8:5-7

Rich with biblical imagery and historical liturgical practices, the marriage liturgy reflects the Anglican understanding of marriage as a sacred union consecrated by God. In examining it, we gain insight into the theological underpinnings of marriage in our Anglican tradition and the ways in which that has been articulated and adapted in the Book of Common Prayer.

It might be helpful to remember here that rituals operate on multiple levels: they are performative acts that symbolize certain beliefs and values of a community and also the ritual enactment of those same beliefs and values. In this case, the marriage liturgy reflects the Church's joy and celebration of the union of two lives joined together by God. And, as the couple acts out the joining of hands and the giving and receiving of rings, we believe that God joins them together.

Love, fidelity, and mutual self-giving are all themes of this service. After the entry processions of the couple and their attendants, which though pragmatic often take on life of their own, the rite begins with the pronouncement of the Church's teaching on marriage. This is followed by the declaration of consent, where the couple publicly affirms their commitment to each other and the gathered community affirms their support of the couple. Here the liturgy reflects the Church's belief that marriage is not only a private relationship between two individuals but also a public expression of faith and commitment set within the context of the wider community. The collect for marriage and readings from Scripture with responses, including a homily, follow.

In the deeply symbolic acts of the joining of hands and giving and receiving of rings, vows are exchanged as the couple promises to love, honor, and cherish each other for better or for worse, for richer or for poorer, in sickness and in health, until parted by death. These vows are accompanied by prayers for God's blessing upon the couple and their life together, including that their life may be a witness to all of God's grace and love.

The service may include the celebration of the Eucharist, sometimes called a Nuptial Mass, underscoring the connection between the marriage covenant and the covenantal relationship between Christ and the Church. The Eucharist serves as a reminder of God's grace and presence in the life of the couple and the congregation, strengthening all for the journey ahead. The liturgy concludes with a blessing over the people and the dismissal, as usual, and the newly married couple process out as witnesses to divine love.

Former Presiding Bishop Michael Curry is fond of saying, "If it's not about love, it's not about God." The Church wrestled for decades with rites to bless love expressed in covenantal relationships beyond opposite-sex ones. The approval within the Episcopal Church of the blessing of same-sex marriages, along with the more recent development of services for covenantal relationships beyond civil marriage, mark significant milestones in the ongoing conversation about inclusion and equality within the denomination. This journey reflects both theological evolution and the Church's engagement with broader societal shifts regarding human sexuality and marriage.

The Episcopal Church's journey towards the blessing of same-sex marriages can be traced back to the 1970s, when LGBTQ+ advocacy groups within the Church began to push for greater recognition and affirmation. However, it wasn't until the early 2000s that the issue gained significant traction within the wider Church.

In 2003, the Episcopal Church ordained and consecrated Gene Robinson as the first openly gay bishop in the Anglican Communion. Robinson's consecration sparked a global debate about the Church's stance on homosexuality and same-sex relationships, highlighting deep theological divisions within the Communion. Despite the controversy and backlash, the Episcopal Church continued to move towards greater inclusion of LGBTQ+ individuals within the life of the Church. In 2012, the Church authorized a provisional rite for the blessing of same-sex unions, allowing priests to officiate blessings for gay and lesbian couples, with the permission of the diocesan bishop. Subsequent General Conventions have approved rites and resolutions that allow all clergy to preside at same-sex weddings, should they choose to, with or without a bishop's permission.

The approved orders of service for same-sex marriages between two people in the Episcopal Church reflect the denomination's commitment to theological integrity and pastoral care for all members of the Church, regardless of sexual orientation or gender identity. While the services follow a traditional liturgical structure, they incorporate language and prayers that affirm the love and commitment of the couple and acknowledge the sacredness of their union before God and the worshipping community.

The Episcopal Church's Standing Commission on Liturgy and Music has further developed orders of service for blessings of non-customary unions. These can be found in the liturgical resources, *I Will Bless, You Will be a Blessing* and *Enriching our Worship 6*. For example, a liturgy has been approved for the blessing of a couple who do not wish to be legally married but who wish to live in a covenantal relationship. Grounded in the theological principle that all individuals are created in the image of God and deserving of love, dignity, and respect, the Episcopal Church continues to discuss the theology of, and liturgical rites for, marriage and covenantal relationships..

To support the couple, the Altar Guild's responsibilities involve careful attention to the liturgical and aesthetic details. Here are key aspects of the Altar Guild's role in weddings:

1. *Communication and Coordination:* Begin by communicating with the clergy, and couple if it is the custom of the parish, to understand their preferences, the liturgical requirements, and any specific elements they wish to incorporate into the ceremony.

2. *Liturgical Colors and Symbols:* The customary liturgical color for weddings is white; however, consult with the clergy and the Church calendar. Coordinate the use of liturgical symbols associated with weddings, such as the exchange of rings and other ceremonial actions. Some parishes even have special kneelers designed for couples to kneel on for the blessing of the marriage—though, one should consult with the couple, especially brides who often wear intricate gowns, if they wish to kneel.

3. *Floral Arrangements and Decorations:* Work with the couple and flower committee or a florist to create arrangements that complement or contribute to the liturgy. Determine if additional decorations are to be used, such as aisle runners, additional floral arrangements, or aisle candles.

4. *Liturgical Books and Vessels:* Ensure that liturgical books, including the Book of Common Prayer, lectionary, altar book, and any special liturgical texts related to weddings, are in place. If Holy Eucharist is part of the wedding, ensure that the appropriate vessels are set up.

5. *Flexibility and Adaptability:* With fewer couples choosing to be married in churches, we all—clergy and laity alike—would do well to be flexible in reasonably accommodating any personalized elements or cultural traditions that the couple wishes to include in the wedding ceremony.

> O gracious and everliving God, you have created humankind in your image: Look mercifully upon [those] who come to you seeking your blessing, and assist them with your grace, that with true fidelity and steadfast love they may honor and keep the promises and vows they make; through Jesus Christ our Savior, who lives and reigns with you in the unity of the Holy Spirit, one God, for ever and ever. Amen.[2]

Ministry to the Sick

> "Are any among you sick? They should call for the elders of the Church and have them pray over them, anointing them with oil in the name of the Lord. The prayer of faith will save the sick, and the Lord will raise them up."
>
> James 5:14-15

The praying and anointing with oil of the sick and dying—called *unction*—was once reserved for the priest alone, in private with the individual and family. This idea is clearly reflected in the rites of Book of Common Prayer. Today, public services of healing have become increasingly common in the liturgical life of our congregations. Also, since the revision of the prayer book in 1979, there have been major medical advancements and new social and pastoral considerations to account for in the liturgical resources of the Church. The prayer book collection includes several forms and a wide variety of prayers

---

2. "I Will Bless You, and You Will Be a Blessing." Revised and Expanded Edition. 2015.

specifically for healing for use by leaders and individuals in the *Book of the Common Prayer, Book of Occasional Services,* and *Enriching our Worship.*

The *ordo,* or pattern of proclamation and response, is found in liturgies for healing, whether in public or private. In the prayer book, a sentence of scripture offers the comfort and assurance of God's presence. In response, prayers are offered for the sick person's healing, comfort, and strength. The prayers often include intercessions for caregivers and family members. Also, the rite allows for a confession of sins and absolution, providing a crucial aspect of healing: a sense of reconciliation with God.

In response to the proclamation of God's mercy and healing grace, the priest may lay hands on the sick person and anoint them with oil. This ritual act is a tangible expression of God's grace and a means of invoking divine healing. Often, the rite includes the sharing of the Holy Communion, which is both a source of spiritual nourishment and, in the case of private rites, a connection to the broader faith community.

The Book of Common Prayer also provides specific prayers for various situations related to illness, such as before surgery, for a swift recovery, and for those suffering from chronic pain. These prayers can be used individually or incorporated into the prayer book rites.

Enriching our Worship 2 offers a broader selection of prayers and the prayer book, enhancing the Church's pastoral care ministry. The most significant advancements in *Enriching our Worship* are the creation of public services of healing and the underlying assumption that lay people share in the ministry of healing as well.

When it comes to the sacramental acts of healing, the Church has provided the rites and resources to adapt our prayers to the specific needs and circumstances of the individuals or community. These rites use language and practices that are inclusive and affirming, and, above all, offer a compassionate presence. A checklist is provided for a public service of healing in the appendix, but the key take-aways for the Altar Guild around healing is to be flexible, inclusive, and pastoral.

> God our healer, whose mercy is like a refining fire: by the lovingkindness of Jesus, heal us and those for whom we pray; that being renewed by you, we may witness your wholeness to our broken world; through Jesus Christ, in the power of the Spirit. Amen. [EOW2, p. 28]

Burial Office

> Jesus said to [Martha], "I am the resurrection and the life. Those who believe in me, even though they die, will live, and everyone who lives and believes in me will never die. Do you believe this?" She said to him, "Yes, Lord, I believe that you are the Messiah, the Son of God, the one coming into the world."

> John 11:25-27

> I believe in... the resurrection of the body and the life everlasting.

> —From the Apostles' Creed [496]

Emphasizing the Christian hope in the victory of life over death through the redemptive work of Christ, this affirmation forms the theological backbone of the burial rites in the Book of Common Prayer. The burial liturgies find their foundation in the Church's understanding of death, resurrection, and the communion of saints. The prayer book includes this note on our burial rites:

> The liturgy for the dead is an Easter liturgy. It finds all meaning in the resurrection. Because Jesus was raised from the dead, we too, shall be raised.

The liturgy, therefore, is characterized by joy, in the certainty that "neither death, nor life, nor angels, nor principalities, nor things present, nor things to come, nor powers, nor height, nor depth, nor anything else in all creation, will be able to separate us from the love of God in Christ Jesus our Lord."

This joy, however, does not make human grief unchristian. The very love we have for each other in Christ brings deep sorrow when we are parted by death. Jesus himself wept at the grave of his friend. So, while we rejoice that one we love has entered into the nearer presence of our Lord, we sorrow in sympathy with those who mourn. [507]

"No one does funeral like the Episcopal Church," a colleague from another denomination texted me after watching a funeral from Washington National Cathedral. Our burial office provides an excellent framework for funerals, both large and small, and it allows for each liturgy to be uniquely crafted to reflect the life of the deceased without excessive novelty.

Usually, the closed coffin (or urn) is placed before the altar, covered with a funeral pall (or veil in the case of an urn). It is becoming increasingly common, however, for the committal and burial to occur first and the service conducted without the remains present. When the body is present, it is customary for the presider to meet it at the church door and proceed it into the church. Sometimes, the Paschal Candle is carried before the coffin or urn by an assisting minister. The Paschal Candle always burns at funerals as a symbol of Christ's resurrection.

There are two liturgies provided in the Book of Common Prayer: Rite One and Rite Two, and there are additional rites provided in *Enriching our Worship*, volumes 2 and 3, including for the Burial of a Child as well as burial rite for someone who does not claim the Christian faith. For our purposes here, we will walk through the order of service using Rite Two.

The service begins with sentences from Scripture, often called the Opening Anthems, which consist of various passages—from John's Gospel, the Book of Job, and Paul's Letter to the Romans—that emphasize the hope of resurrection. The Opening Anthems immediately focus the congregation on the Christian hope of eternal life.

The Collect gathers the individual prayers of the congregation and summarizes the themes of the service, asking for God's presence and comfort for those who mourn and interceding for the deceased's soul. A selection of passages from the Old and New Testaments are read, chosen to reflect the themes of hope, resurrection, and God's everlasting love. Eulogies and / or a homily follow. These brief reflections should focus on the life of the deceased as it relates to the hope of the resurrection.

The Apostles' Creed is then recited by the congregation and a series of prayers are offered for the deceased, their family, and all who mourn. The prayers are quite different between Rites One and Two. *Enriching our Worship 3* offers additional options.

The Eucharist may then be celebrated. Here it serves as a reminder that this sacred meal is a foretaste of the heavenly banquet "in that kingdom where there is no death but the fullness of joy with all the saints." [498]

Recalling again our discussions of ritual: at the Commendation we both acknowledge of trust and belief in the eternal presence of God and in that moment commit the soul of the deceased into God's care. The ancient hymn, the *Kontakion*, is sung or recited: "Give rest, O Christ, to your servant with your saints; where sorrow and pain are no more, neither sighing, but life everlasting." [499] As the body is borne from the church, a hymn or canticle is sung or said.

The committal, if not done earlier, brings the liturgy of the Church to the final resting place of the deceased. It serves as a final act of farewell and a reminder of the promise of resurrection. This moment acknowledges the physical reality of death—*earth to earth, ashes to ashes, dust to dust*—while expressing hope in the resurrection. A closing prayer seeks God's blessing and peace for all present, asking for strength and comfort in the days ahead.

The service emphasizes God's compassion and care for both the deceased and the living. The communal nature of the service highlights the support of the faith community. Members of an Altar Guild play a crucial role in support of funeral services—a pastoral ministry that can provide comfort for grieving families and congregants through your careful preparation. The role of the Altar Guild for funerals involves various responsibilities:

1. *Communication and Coordination:* Work closely with the officiating clergy to align parish customary with any unique considerations for the funeral service.

2. *Liturgical Colors and Symbols:* White, the color used for liturgies of the resurrection, is usually used. Some congregations may still use purple or black. Coordinate the use of liturgical symbols associated with funerals, such as the pall, funeral processional cross or paschal candle that provide visual representation of the Christian hope of the resurrection.

3. *Floral Arrangements:* Work with the family and flower committee or a florist to create floral arrangements. Consider additional decorations, such as memorial candles or additional floral arrangements.

4. *Liturgical Books and Vessels*: Ensure that liturgical books, including the Book of Common Prayer, hymnals, and any special liturgical texts related to funerals, are in place. If Holy Eucharist is part of the funeral, ensure that the vessels used are clean and in place.

5. *Flexibility and Adaptability:* Funerals require the utmost pastoral sensitivity. Be flexible in reasonably accommodating any personalized elements or cultural traditions that the family

wishes to include. If it is important to them, it should be important to you.

> Gracious God, you alone are the source of all life, may your life-giving Spirit flow through us, so that we may be ministers of your compassion to one another; in our sorrow give us the calm of your peace, kindle our hope, and in your good time, let our grief give way to joy, through Jesus Christ our Deliverer. Amen. [EOW3, 62]

Other Pastoral Rites

While the last two rites discussed usually will not involve direct involvement by the Altar Guild, it is helpful, as we have throughout this book, to place the ministry within a larger historical, theological, and liturgical context. These two rites are: Thanksgiving for the Birth and Adoption of a Child and Reconciliation of a Penitent.

The order for the *Thanksgiving for the Birth and Adoption of a Child* is grounded in the belief that children are a precious gift from God, entrusted to the care of their parents and the wider community. It acknowledges the joy and responsibility that comes with the gift of new life and affirms the importance of raising children within the context of faith and community.

The thanksgiving for the birth or adoption of a child is typically held within the context of a regular worship service, such as the Sunday Eucharist. The family presents the child to the congregation, where they are welcomed with prayers, blessings, and words of encouragement.

The liturgy includes prayers of thanksgiving for the safe delivery of the child, prayers for the health and well-being of the child and parents, and prayers for wisdom and grace in the task of parenting. Scripture readings may be selected that speak to the themes of new life, God's faithfulness, and the blessings of family and community.

One of the central elements of the service is the presentation of the child to God and the community. This symbolic act represents the parents' commitment to raising the child in the love of the Lord and represents the congregation's commitment to supporting and nurturing the child in the life of faith.

The officiant may offer a special blessing for the child, invoking God's grace and protection upon them as they grow and develop. The congregation may also join in offering prayers and blessings for the child and family, expressing their love and support for their journey together.

The service concludes with a prayer of thanksgiving and a blessing for the family, sending them forth with the assurance of God's presence and grace in their lives, surrounded by the love and support of the community.

There are two rites for *Reconciliation of a Penitent* in the Book of Common Prayer. Both forms maintain the core elements of confession, absolution, and penance, but they offer different formats to accommodate personal preference and pastoral need.

Form One begins with the penitent approaching the priest, who acts *in persona christi*. The penitent confesses their sins using a set form of words. The priest then offers counsel, assigns a prayerful or restorative action of penance, and pronounces absolution. The form includes an explicit acknowledgment of the seriousness of sin, the mercy of God, and the assurance of forgiveness. The absolution formula emphasizes the authority given to priests to forgive sins, echoing Jesus' words to his disciples in the Gospel of John: "If you forgive the sins of any, they are forgiven them; if you retain the sins of any, they are retained." (20:23).

Form Two offers a more flexible and conversational approach and is based more on the Eastern rite of reconciliation. It begins with an opening prayer, followed by the penitent's confession in their own words. This form allows for more interaction between the priest and penitent, including opportunities for pastoral guidance. The absolution and the assignment of penance are similar to Form One, but the language is simpler and more direct.

This sacramental act offered here is more than a declaration; it is an efficacious sign of God's mercy, restoring the penitent to a state of grace. The rite also includes elements of pastoral care with acts of penance intended to help the penitent amend their life and grow closer to God. This reflects the holistic understanding of sin and reconciliation in the Episcopal tradition, which sees sin as damaging relationships with God, others, and oneself, and reconciliation as the restoration of those relationships.

The *Reconciliation of a Penitent* is typically conducted in a private setting, ensuring confidentiality and allowing for a candid and honest confession. This privacy underscores the personal nature of the sacrament and respects the dignity of the penitent.

Conclusion

The pastoral rites of the Book of Common Prayer provide profound spiritual support, marking life's signal moments with grace and dignity. Rooted in scripture and tradition, they serve as anchors of hope, celebrate life's joys, ease its sorrows, and underscore the continuity of God's love and care.

The Altar Guild's role in these liturgies is more than just liturgical: it is pastoral. You can share in the joys and sorrows of these transitional life moments and have the privilege to be witnesses to God's transforming grace at work.

Almighty and eternal God, so draw our hearts to thee, so guide our minds, so fill our imaginations, so control our wills, that we may be wholly thine, utterly dedicated unto thee; and then use us, we pray thee, as thou wilt, and always to thy glory and the welfare of thy people; through our Lord and Savior Jesus Christ. Amen. [832]

CHAPTER THIRTEEN

SPECIAL SERVICES

Lord, you give the great commission:
"Heal the sick and preach the word."
Lest the Church neglect its mission
and the Gospel go unheard,
help us witness to your purpose
with renewed integrity;
with the Spirit's gifts empowers us
for the work of ministry.[1]

O ur attention turns now to special services that occur in our congregations: bishop's visitations, celebrations of new ministry, and ordinations. Since they are occasional, they can often be anxiety producing. It is hoped that by learning more about the context, sacristans will be more at ease and feel empowered and better enabled to offer support and embrace the opportunity to renew and celebrate the mission of the Church through these liturgies.

A Bishop's Visit

"Transcendent and sublime," is how the bishop described her visit to one of the parishes of the diocese. The Rector "crafted an elegant and powerful liturgy. We welcomed eleven new Episcopalians through the sacrament of Confirmation and Reception. The music was amazing, the hospitality was unparalleled." About the mitre worn? The head sacristan crafted it himself to

---

1. Rowthorn, Jeffrey. "Lord, you give the great commission." (New York: Church Hymnal Corporation, 1985), 528.

match the parish's historic vestments and "it fit perfectly in all of the ways."[2]

Unparalleled hospitality. This is something towards which all our churches should always strive. However, hospitality is of unique importance when a bishop visits. According to the Canons of the Episcopal Church, the bishop is required to visit each parish in their diocese at least once every three years. In some dioceses, bishop visits are an annual event. The visitation of a bishop is deeply rooted in tradition and history and is a significant, if not anxiety-producing, occasion.

Bishop Paul Marshall, former Bishop of Bethlehem (PA), calls a bishop a wandering minstrel, host, and guest during visitation liturgies.[3] As the bishop moves throughout the diocese under their care, the people gather to celebrate the Eucharist along with the rites of Confirmation, Reception, and Reaffirmation, as we discussed in an earlier chapter. In their role as wandering minstrel, the bishop also shares the stories of that diocese in all the parishes and congregations, hoping to be both a symbol of, and to seek to effect, unity.

On these visits, a bishop is also both a host and a guest. A bishop is a guest because, even if at cathedrals in most cases, your parish is not where the bishop presides with regularity on Sundays; the bishop does not always know the idiosyncrasies of the liturgy or the pastoral needs of the congregation. They are like a host because all congregations are ultimately under the missional and pastoral care of the bishop; thus, it is expected by our prayer book that the bishop will preside and preach at these visitation liturgies

Bishop's visits often involve special liturgies, ceremonies, and celebrations. Here are some key preparations that the Altar Guild might undertake for a bishop's visit:

---

2. Schofield-Broadbent, Carrie. (2024, June 12) "Last night was transcendent and sublime." [Facebook] https://www.facebook.com/bishopcarriesb. Retrieved 16 June 2024.

3. Marhsall, Paul. *The Bishop is Coming! A Practical Guide for Bishops and Congregations.* (New York: Church Publishing, 2007), 3.

1. *The Bishop's Customary:* The Altar Guild should communicate with the Rector or clergy-in-charge well in advance of the bishop's visit to discuss any specific liturgical preferences or requirements, and to address logistical details. Some bishops have very detailed customaries and preferences that might differ from the usual practice of your parish; accommodating this is both a sign of respect and an opportunity for education, as you will learn the thinking and spirituality that, hopefully, undergirds these requests.

2. *Liturgical Colors and Vestments:* Determine the liturgical colors for the day based on the liturgical calendar or any special occasion. The bishop often will bring her or his own liturgical vestments, such as the cope, mitre, and crozier; however, this is a good opportunity to make sure if the parish's vestments will be used that they are cleaned and in good order.

3. *Prepare the altar and sanctuary:*

   - *Paraments:* Select and arrange paraments that align with the liturgical season or the specific occasion.

   - *Floral arrangements:* Coordinate with the flower committee or arrange for special floral decorations that complement the liturgical colors and create a festive atmosphere.

   - *Prepare the bishop's chair:* Ensure that the presider's chair, if applicable, is appropriately positioned prominently in the sanctuary.

4. *Liturgical elements:*

   - *Liturgical books:* Ensure that liturgical books, including the Book of Common Prayer, hymnal, altar book and any additional resources needed for the special service, are in place and in good condition.

   - *Liturgical vessels:* Prepare the chalice and paten, etc. for Holy Eucharist, ensuring they are clean and polished. Consult with your clergy and the bishop's customary to determine if any specific vessels are to be used (i.e. chrism).

5. *Prepare for special rites or Confirmations:* If the bishop is conducting confirmations or other special rites, work closely with your clergy as needed to coordinate the logistics, including the placement of candidates, chrism, and any additional liturgical elements.

6. *Review Liturgical Details:* Conduct a final review of the liturgical details with the clergy, ensuring that everyone involved in the service is on the same page regarding the order of worship, special instructions, and any variations from the typical liturgy.

Not all sacristans should be expected to hand-craft a mitre for the bishop, and many bishops might not appreciate such a gesture. However, the Altar Guild plays a crucial role in preparing for these visits and ensuring unparalleled hospitality for both the bishop and the congregation.

> O God, our heavenly Father, who raised up your faithful servant to be a bishop and pastor in your Church and to feed your flock: Give abundantly to all pastors the gifts of your Holy Spirit, that they may minister in your household as true servants of Christ and stewards of your divine mysteries; through Jesus Christ our Lord, who lives and reigns with you and the Holy Spirit, one God, for ever and ever. Amen. [248]

Celebration of New Ministry

> A new heart I will give you, and a new spirit I will put within you, and I will remove from your body the heart of stone and give you a heart of flesh. I will put my spirit within you and make you follow my statutes and be careful to observe

my ordinances. Then you shall live in the land that I gave
to your ancestors, and you shall be my people, and I will be
your God. (Ezekiel 34:26-28)

During my time as Canon Liturgist for the Bishop of Long Island,
I was present for about two dozen institutions of new rectors and
other ministers. While usually carefully following our customary, each
liturgy reflected the diversity of the congregation, clergy-person, and
regional culture. These services were often joy-filled and signal events
in the life of the congregation.

The Celebration of New Ministry marks the beginning of a new
chapter in the life of a parish or congregation. The order for the liturgy
can be found in the Book of Common Prayer or in *Enriching Our
Worship 4*, which provides a renewed order. Both orders are set within
the context of the Eucharist at which the bishop usually presides, yet
the structure and theological implications vary.

The focal point of the Celebration of New Ministry in the
Book of Common Prayer is the giving of symbols of ministry by
the bishop, representatives of diocesan clergy, church wardens,
and members of the congregation. The bishop presents water
as a symbol of the bishop's historic role at the initiation of new
Christians and the new rector or other minister, if a priest, to share
in this role and help the bishop to "baptize in obedience to our
Lord" [561]. Diocesan clergy present the Canons of the Episcopal
Church as a symbol of the priest's role to "share in the councils of
the diocese" [562] Wardens present keys and other representatives
present a Bible, bread and wine, a stole, prayer book, and oil of
healing; all symbols of the ministry and roles of the priest within
the congregation.

It is helpful to note here that other appropriate symbols of ministry
may be given, but these should be limited since this is a liturgical
act. As we have established, Episcopalians embrace incarnational
theology, and the giving symbolic gifts is, in part, about real human

connections, which we know Jesus shared. That said, the giving of other gifts, such as welcome baskets, gag gifts, barbecue grills, etc.—all of which I've witnessed—are best left for the reception after as they do not enhance the symbolism of the ritual.

One of the challenges of the order in the Book of Common Prayer is the ecclesiastical implications of the liturgy. The bishop concludes the presentation of gifts by saying, "let all these be signs of the ministry which is mine and yours in this place" [562], notably leaving out the participation of the congregation and, possibly unintentionally, disconnecting the congregation from the ministry of all the baptized.

Enriching our Worship 4 sought to remedy this. The liturgy, with the institution of the new rector or other minister, is set again within the context of the Holy Eucharist but now including the Renewal of Baptismal Vows. The presentation of gifts is no longer the focal point. The giving of symbols of ministry is spread throughout the liturgy. The Bible is presented before the lessons are read, the bread and wine as the altar is prepared, and the water as the congregation prepares to renew their baptismal vows. This could be considered the central moment of the liturgy, at the baptismal font, when the bishop asks the assembly, "Will you work together as partner in the mission of the Church, to reconcile all people to God through Christ?" [EOW4, p.6] The emphasis of this liturgy is on the renewal of the ministry of the whole congregation and the partnership between priest and people that stems from the baptismal font and continues as the assembly gathers around the holy table. And, then, together, they offer ministry as the Body of Christ.

Regardless of the rite chosen, the Altar Guild will play a vital role in preparing for this liturgy. Here are some considerations for the Altar Guild in the celebration of a new ministry:

1. *Communication and coordination:* Well in advance, begin communicating with the clergy person, the bishop's office (if

applicable), and other relevant parties involved in the service. Understand any specific liturgical requirements or preferences for the celebration.

2. *Paraments and vestments:*
   - *Liturgical colors:* Determine the appropriate liturgical colors for the day based on the liturgical calendar or any special considerations. Coordinate with the new clergy person or the bishop's office to ensure alignment with the occasion.
   - *Clergy vestments:* Ensure that the clergy person's vestments, including chasuble, stole, and other liturgical attire, are clean and prepared for the service.

3. *Floral Arrangements and Decorations:*
   - *Coordinate with flower committee:* Work with the flower committee or florist to create floral arrangements that complement the liturgical colors and contribute to the festive atmosphere.
   - *Special decorations:* Consider any additional decorations, such as banners or symbolic elements, to mark the celebration of the new ministry.

4. *Liturgical elements:*
   - *Liturgical books:* Confirm that liturgical books, including the Book of Common Prayer, hymnal, altar book and any special liturgical texts, are in place and accessible.
   - *Liturgical vessels:* Prepare the chalice and paten and other vessels for Holy Eucharist, ensuring they are clean and polished. Confirm what other vessels might be needed.

5. *Special rites and ceremonies:*
   - *Processional elements:* Coordinate any processions or ceremonial actions associated with the institution.
   - *Ceremonial gifts:* It is often part of the rite that ceremonial gifts are given. These include a flagon of water for baptism, a

stole, bread and wine, oil for healing, a bible and prayer book, keys to the church, and a copy of the canons. These symbols should be large enough to be visible. A table or two will be needed for these gifts.

The Celebration of a New Ministry is a significant event in the life of our parish communities. While usually focused on the specific ministry of one person, it is an opportunity for the whole congregation to celebrate baptismal ministry to which all are called: "to proclaim by word and example the Good News of God in Christ." [305]

Grant, Lord God, to all who have been baptized into the death and resurrection of your Son Jesus Christ, that, as we have put away the old life of sin, so we may be renewed in the spirit of our minds, and live in righteousness and true holiness; through Jesus Christ our Lord, who lives and reigns with you, in the unity of the Holy Spirit, one God, now and for ever. Amen. [252]

Ordinations

Q. Who are the ministers of the Church?
A. The ministers of the Church are lay persons, bishops, priests, and deacons.

From the Catechism of the Book
of Common Prayer [855-6]

From the Greek *laikos,* meaning "of the people," the laity is a cornerstone of the Church's life and mission. Lay people contribute in myriad ways, from worship and teaching to service and leadership. Their involvement reflects the biblical principle of the "priesthood of all believers" (see 1 Peter 2:9) and underscores the collaborative nature of the Church's mission.

Q. What is the ministry of the laity?

A. The ministry of lay persons is to represent Christ and his Church; to bear witness to him wherever they may be; and, according to the gifts given them, to carry on Christ's work of reconciliation in the world; and to take their place in the life, worship, and governance of the Church.

While much of the ministry, like the Altar Guild, in the Church is done by lay persons, our attention turns here to the ordination rites of the Church. In the Anglican tradition, the three orders of ordained ministry are the Diaconate, the Priesthood or Presbyterate, and the Episcopate. While each of these orders are distinct and unique, they are sequential: that is to say, to be ordained a priest, one must be ordained a deacon first and both in sequence before being ordained to the episcopate, if called and elected. The revival of the diaconate as a vocation in and of itself, without seeking ordination to the priesthood, has been significant in the life of the Church and has been the subject of much conversation and debate over the last half-century.

The ordination rites in the Book of Common Prayer are rich in tradition and theology and reflect the Episcopal Church's commitment to maintaining the apostolic ministry and the distinct roles within it. These rites not only consecrate individuals for specific ministry but also strengthen the bonds of unity and continuity within the Church. Here we will look at each rite separately.

Q. What is the ministry of a deacon?

A. The ministry of a deacon is to represent Christ and his Church, particularly as a servant of those in need; and to assist bishops and priests in the proclamation of the Gospel and the administration of the sacraments.

Deacons are ordained to serve as servants of the Church. The ordination of deacons is seen as a tangible expression of the Church's commitment to serve the world in the name of Christ.

The liturgy prescribed in the Book of Common Prayer begins with the presentation of the candidates to the bishop by representatives of the diocese. The candidate for ordination takes the Oath of Conformity, stating that they will conform to the "doctrine, discipline and worship" of the Episcopal Church. The Litany of Ordinations is sung (or said), the collect used at ordinations is prayed, Scripture read, and a sermon given. The lessons chosen for the day come from those appointed in the ordination rite or from those appointed for the feast day, if applicable.

Following the Sermon and Nicene Creed, the bishop examines the candidates, where questions are posed to ensure their commitment to the diaconate's service-oriented nature. The hymn *Veni Creator Spiritus* or *Veni Sancte Spiritus* is then sung. The bishop offers the prayer of Consecration of a Deacon and lays hands on each candidate, invoking the Holy Spirit to empower them for ministry.

The new deacons are now vested according to the Order of Deacons. A deacon's stole is traditionally worn diagonally across the body, symbolizing their role as servants of Christ and the Church. A deacon may also be vested in a dalmatic, which is a long, sleeved tunic that goes over the alb and stole. Believed to originate in Dalmatia (now Croatia) in the 3rd century, it became a popular secular garment of upper-class women in Rome in about the 4th century. Over time, it became associated with the order of deacons and by the 9th century it had become quite ornate and made to match the liturgical colors.

The bishop then presents a Bible to each deacon, underscoring their duty to proclaim the Gospel. The service culminates in the Eucharist, with the newly ordained deacons taking on their proper roles of preparing the altar, assisting in the distribution of Communion, and offering the concluding dismissal.

Q. What is the ministry of a priest or presbyter?

A. The ministry of a priest is to represent Christ and his Church, particularly as pastor to the people; to share with the bishop in the overseeing of the Church; to proclaim the Gospel; to administer the sacraments; and to bless and declare pardon in the name of God.

Priests are set apart by the Church to preach, celebrate the sacraments, and provide pastoral care to the people of God. Priest and presbyter are often used interchangeably, though be cautious of the possible theological and ecclesiological nuances. The word *presbyter* comes from the Greek word *presbyteros*, which can be literally translated as "old man," or more commonly, "elder." [Think of our friends in the Presbyterian Church—they are a church of elders, whereas the Episcopal Church is a church with bishops.] The English word *priest* derives from the same Greek word, *presbyteros*, and links the New Testament understanding of "elder" with the ancient Hebrew priesthood, according to the order of Melchizedek (Genesis 14:18-20).

As we have seen many times before, the ritual of the ordination both declares what the Church believes about the priesthood and enacts it through the liturgy with great care, emphasizing the priest's sacramental and pastoral role. It would be helpful here to walk through the ordination liturgy.

As with deacons, the candidates are presented to the bishop, who again sign the Oath of Conformity. The Litany for Ordinations is sung, Scripture proclaimed, sermon offered, and Creed recited. At the time of the Consecration of the Priest, the bishop, joined by the other priests present, lay hands on the candidates. Sometimes called affectionally *the holy huddle*, this signifies the communal nature of the priesthood.

The newly ordained priests are vested according to the order. In some dioceses, priests are just given a stole, which is worn vertically rather than diagonally like a deacon. In most cases, a priest is vested with a stole and chasuble, symbolizing their role in presiding over the Eucharist and other sacraments. Again, the bishop presents a bible to the new priests to remind them of their call to preach the Word of God.

Occasionally, the bishop anoints the hands of the new priests with chrism. Anointing with oil stems from the Old Testament and indicates that someone, or something, is being set apart for a sacred task. This anointing signifies that the hands of the newly ordained priests are being prepared for the sacred duties and vessels which will be part of their ministry, for example, offering the bread and the wine, anointing the sick, and blessing people. In some cases, a chalice and paten are also then presented to the new priest, emphasizing their roles in the celebration of the Eucharist.

Holy Communion follows, with the new priests presiding alongside the bishop, demonstrating their new role in leading the community in worship. At the conclusion of the liturgy, the newly ordained offer the final blessing.

Q. What is the ministry of a bishop?

A. The ministry of a bishop is to represent Christ and his Church, particularly as apostle, chief priest, and pastor of a diocese; to guard the faith, unity, and discipline of the whole Church; to proclaim the Word of God; to act in Christ's name for the reconciliation of the world and the building up of the Church; and to ordain others to continue Christ's ministry.

The Episcopate is the third order of ordained ministry within the Anglican tradition. Bishops are ordained to provide oversight, leadership, and unity within the Church. The ordination of bishops is regarded as a sign of continuity with the apostolic tradition, as bishops are seen as successors to the apostles in the ministry of oversight and pastoral care.

The ordination of bishops often take place in the cathedral or space large enough to host the liturgy, since it is one that involves the whole diocese and representatives of the Church. The Presiding Bishop, or a designated bishop, serves as chief consecrator and is joined, according to canons, by at least two co-consecrating bishops. Deacons, priests, and lay people from throughout the diocese and Church participate in the liturgy, as well.

Similar to other ordination rites, the bishop-elect is first presented to the presiding bishop. In this case, testimonials of election and consents to the election are then read, representing the larger nature of this role. Again, the litany is sung, Scripture proclaimed, and a sermon preached. The prayer book presumes that the ordination occurs on a Sunday or other major feast; however, this is not common practice. Lessons from Scripture are chosen from the day or from those suggested in the order itself.

After the hymn that follows the sermon, the co-consecrating bishops share in the examination of the bishop, who is called to be the "chief priest and pastor" [518]. As a "guardian of the Church's faith" [519], the bishop-elect leads the recitation of the Nicene Creed.

Here follows the Consecration of the Bishop. During the singing of the *Veni Creator Spiritus* or *Veni Sancte Spiritus*, the bishop-elect kneels before the chief consecrator and all the bishops present gather for the laying on of hands. The prayer of consecration is largely based on the 3rd century prayer from the *Apostolic Tradition*.

The bishop is then vested according to the order of bishops. Most commonly, bishops are vested in stole, chasuble, and mitre; though some retain the tradition of wearing rochet and chimere. Symbols of the office—pectoral cross, ring, and crozier—are presented. The chief consecrator presents a bible and then presents the bishop to assembly, who offer "their acclamation and applause" [522]. As a ritual act, this demonstrates their pledge of support and encouragement for the bishop that they elected some months earlier. The new bishop bids the peace and the congregation shares in the Holy Eucharist.

The *Book of Occasional Services* provides for the seating of the bishop, in their *cathedra* (or "chair"), a symbol of their role as presider over the Church in that place and their responsibility to serve as chief teacher. In the Middle Ages, the bishop was seen as the ruler of the diocese and the *cathedra* often took on the image of a throne; we would do well to stay away from that imagery today. This rite might occur during the ordination liturgy or at a separate day and time.

Ordinations are times of great celebration in the life of the Church. Some parishes may be used to having ordinations held there and for some it may be a rarity, once in a lifetime even. Here is an overview of the Altar Guild's role in ordination services:

1. *Communication:*
   - *Collaborate with clergy:* Work closely with the clergy who will be directly involved in the ordination to ensure a seamless coordination of the liturgy.
   - *Review the bishop's customary:* In advance, discuss with your clergy person, or bishop's office if applicable, any specific liturgical requirements, preferences, or guidelines for the ordination liturgy.
2. *Liturgical colors, vestments, and symbols:*
   - *Determine liturgical colors:* Identify the liturgical colors appropriate for the specific ordination service, which may vary based on the liturgical calendar or custom of the diocese. It is common that red or white vestments are used.
   - *Select appropriate paraments and vestments:* Coordinate altar hangings that align with the liturgical colors and confirm that the vestments for the ordinands and other clergy are clean, in good condition, and prepared for the service.
3. *Liturgical elements and vessels:*
   - *Prepare liturgical books:* Ensure that liturgical books, including the Book of Common Prayer, hymnals, altar book, and any special liturgical texts related to ordination, are in place.
   - *Prepare Vessels:* Ensure the chalices and patens and other vessels are polished and prepared for the Holy Eucharist.

4. *Set-up of sanctuary:*

- *Enhanced setup:* Consider any enhancements (i.e. reserved seating, extra setting, etc.) to the typical setup that are appropriate for the ordination. Make sure that the vestments and other symbols of ministry to be given are conveniently placed.
- *Bishop's chair:* Ensure that the bishop's chair is appropriately positioned in the sanctuary and visible for the act of presiding.
- *Floral arrangements:* Coordinate with the flower committee or florist to create floral arrangements that complement the liturgical colors and enhance the liturgical space.

Conclusion

The visit of a bishop, the institution of a rector or other pastoral leader, and ordinations can be times of heightened stress for the Altar Guild. Good communication and preparation, though always important, is even more crucial here. Above all, remember that these are occasions of great celebration and joy in the life of the Church and are visible symbols of the living God who is at work transforming lives and renewing the mission of the Church.

O God of unchangeable power and eternal light: Look favorably on your whole Church, that wonderful and sacred mystery; by the effectual working of your providence, carry out in tranquility the plan of salvation; let the whole world see and know that things which were cast down are being raised up, and things which had grown old are being made new, and that all things are being brought to their perfection by him through whom all things were made, your Son Jesus Christ our Lord; who lives and reigns with you, in the unity of the Holy Spirit, one God, for ever and ever. Amen. [515]

CHAPTER FOURTEEN

CONTEMPORARY CONSIDERATIONS

For though I am free with respect to all, I have made myself a slave to all, so that I might gain all the more. To the Jews I became as a Jew, in order to gain Jews. To those under the law I became as one under the law (though I myself am not under the law) so that I might gain those under the law. To those outside the law I became as one outside the law (though I am not outside God's law but am within Christ's law) so that I might gain those outside the law. To the weak I became weak, so that I might gain the weak. I have become all things to all people, that I might by all means save some. I do it all for the sake of the gospel, so that I might become a partner in it.

1 Corinthians 9: 19-23

Blessed are the flexible, for they shall bend but not break!

Contemporary Proverb

"This just doesn't look right," Nancy said, almost itchy from the apparent chaos of the decorations. She wasn't wrong; it did look a little odd.

- Two large cut fresh flower arrangements on the reredos behind the altar
- Two faux Christmas trees that would have been serious obstacles to liturgical movement
- Six seemingly random-placed poinsettias in the Chancel
- Fresh greens with white and red carnations carefully arranged around half of the top of the pulpit

This was the checklist for the Christmas decorations assembled on December 15, 2020, at St. Paul's Church in Rochester, New York. "OK, now, let's see how that looks on screen," became a mantra of sorts as a few of us, masked, gathered around a computer, adjusting the camera to different angles only to readjust the decorations.

There was to be no in-person worship for Christmas 2020, and a recording of our online Christmas Festival of Lessons and Carols would take place over the course of the next few days. By Christmas Eve, the cut flowers from the pulpit and reredos had been turned into smaller arrangements and were delivered, along with the poinsettias, to our *more* home-bound parishioners.

The Church sure has done a lot of adapting in recent years, and not just with flowers. We've become proficient in Zoom and Google Meet; we've invested in cameras for worship and meeting spaces; we've embraced the idea of work from home; we've learned what traditions are of great value and which ones we can let go of; and, we've recognized the importance of staying connected as a faithful community. Also, the COVID-19 pandemic taught us a lot about the need to be flexible and creative. This chapter is a discussion of two areas that, although important before 2020, have taken on new relevance since: online worship and health and safety.

Online Worship

Today, for better or worse depending on your perspective, many churches have embraced technology to extend their reach beyond the physical confines of the building. While a few churches put the cameras away, live-streamed and/or recorded services have become increasingly popular, allowing congregants to participate in the worship of their faith community remotely. This creates both challenges and opportunities for the Altar Guild.

We have seen how the Altar Guild plays a key role in creating an inclusive and welcoming environment for all worshippers and this can extend now to whether those worshippers are present on-site or online. By actively engaging with the parish's media team, the Altar Guild can contribute to a more seamless and spiritually enriching experience for both the on-site and remote congregations. What follows are just some of the considerations for the Altar Guild in the context of live-streamed church services.

An Altar Guild member or two may need to be assigned to work in coordination with technical teams to ensure that liturgical vessels and vestments, as well as seasonal decorations, are positioned in a way that complements the camera setup. Attention to lighting, angles, and background aesthetics is newly important. The use of colors, well-coordinated appointments and decorations, and an organized sanctuary with minimized distractions enhance the visual experience for online viewers, as well as those present on-site. Not only do the Altar Guild members need to take the proverbial step back, but they might also need to think like a television producer and check the view on the screen.

An Altar Guild member might also wish to work with media teams to ensure that any digital content aligns with the church season or possibly even coordinates with the vestments, paraments, and other liturgical items used. For example, it might be possible for a graphic artist to create digital symbols or icons drawn from art in the sanctuary thereby connecting the online community with the physical space of the church.

It is crucial here to mention the mutuality in this and that this is not just the role of the Altar Guild. A good parish technical team, along with the clergy, would listen to the perspectives and needs of the Altar Guild; many of its members could be a valuable resource with both a creative and liturgically sensitive eye for detail.

The Altar Guild's role has long focused on the aspects of the physical church environment with customs, practices, and routines that are well-rooted. By balancing the traditional aspects of their role with the demands of the digital age, the Altar Guild can serve as both custodians of sacred tradition and creative leaders who can adapt to meet changing needs. This, indeed, can be very helpful to the life of the congregation.

Health and Safety

While the focus of the Altar Guild is primarily on preparing the sanctuary for the liturgies of the Church, there is an increased focus on all leaders to consider health and safety. For the purpose of this book, this applies to both the well-being of both Altar Guild members and the congregation.

The likelihood that we will face another pandemic is not slim. Today, there is a heightened awareness among many people about the spreading of viruses, even during the yearly cold and flu season. In light of these health concerns, Altar Guild members should be well-informed about good hygiene practices, including handwashing, sanitization, and any specific guidelines related to public health. As we saw with COVID-19, this guidance and practice might vary from region to region, diocese to diocese, and parish to parish. Consideration should be given to the tasteful and careful placement of hand-sanitizer, masks, etc. While these might need to be easily accessible, they should not distract from the liturgical space and their use should not become para-liturgical actions (i.e. a ceremonial spritzing of hand-sanitizer around the altar).

Along the lines of health, members of the Altar Guild, and the congregation as a whole, may have allergies or sensitivities to cleaning products, incense, or flowers, as well as the more obvious allergies to bread with gluten and to alcohol. Altar Guild leaders should be considerate of these potential issues and, especially regarding Communion, work with the clergy to ensure all may be reasonably included and accommodated. It bears repeating that gluten-free hosts should not be mixed with bread with gluten; similarly, non-alcoholic wine and wine with alcohol should be clearly labeled. While it is helpful for these to be kept in distinct vessels, please remember to treat both with equal dignity and respect as elements of the Eucharist. Though not common, some parishes use gluten-free bread and non-alcoholic wine solely, with the permission of the diocesan bishop when needed.

While these above examples look at the congregation as a whole, our attention turns now to mainly the Altar Guild. Members may need to lift and move heavy or awkward items, such as crosses, candlesticks, candelabras, frontals, chairs, or other liturgical items. Proper lifting techniques can help prevent strains and injuries. The use of ergonomic tools, such as standing mats, might help in the sacristy.

Cleaning and polishing materials used by the Altar Guild may contain chemicals. Members should be aware of proper handling procedures, use protective gear like gloves, and ensure adequate ventilation when working with these substances. Likewise, regular maintenance of equipment, such as ladders or scaffolding used for decorating, is crucial. Inspecting these tools for wear and tear can prevent accidents and injuries.

Altar Guild members move around the church a lot, especially during the setup and preparation of services. They should be mindful of potential hazards, such as slippery floors, steps and other tripping hazards and take necessary precautions to prevent slips and falls. The edge of steps can be discreetly taped for better visibility and any decorative rugs can be secured. Use caution on stairs, especially when carrying items; and avoid walking backwards down steps. There are plenty of stories of people getting hurt because they were in a rush.

Accidents happen and having individuals, or a plan for, who can provide immediate first aid can make a significant difference in the outcome of an injury. This might be the reminder you need to purchase a functional and well-stocked first aid kit to keep in the sacristy.

Here seems like a good place to share this story. It was during the third week of Advent when the Altar Guild director was returning cleaned and pressed linens to her parish's sacristy. As she looked up the short staircase into the sanctuary, she saw part of the Advent wreath engulfed in flames. Preventing greater disaster, she was able to extinguish the small conflagration, but the damage was already done. By Sunday, the wreath was re-assembled with fresh candles (some even burned down to give the appearance of time-passing); by Advent the next year, the decision was made to use re-fillable oil candles and an artificial wreath.

Candles are often an integral part of our liturgies. Altar Guild members should double or triple check that they have been extinguished. It might be helpful to consider switching to oil candles out of safety, convenience, and cost consideration. Sacristans should be trained in fire safety protocols, including proper candle handling, regular and emergency extinguishing procedures, and awareness of fire exits.

Sadly, we live in a violent and unpredictable world and, as we have seen, churches are not free from shootings and other violence, theft, and natural disasters. Altar Guild leadership should be part of conversations with clergy and lay leadership about emergency protocols and plans. Again, having a plan for how to respond in the unlikely event of such an emergency will make a significant difference and will provide a sense of safety in this sacred space.

Finally, and of utmost importance, is the consideration of Safe Church training. Training by leadership and volunteers in sexual harassment and child abuse prevention is a requirement of the Episcopal Church. Safe Church and similar programs are designed to help us live into our baptismal covenant to respect the dignity of all people, most especially to protect the most vulnerable in our communities. To learn more about this, speak to your clergy or your diocesan leadership.

There are probably plenty of other considerations that our parish Altar Guilds make with regard to the health and safety of members and the whole congregation. If you can imagine it, it's probably good to have a conversation about it. Above all, establishing clear communication channels within the Altar Guild and with clergy and other church leadership is essential for ensuring that everyone is aware of safety protocols, emergency procedures, and any specific health concerns in the parish community.

Live without fear: your Creator has made you holy, has always protected you, and loves you as a mother. Go in peace to follow the good road and may God's blessing be with you always. Amen.

Saint Clare of Assisi [EOW, 71]

AFTERWORD

We thank Thee, O Lord, that Thou has permitted us to serve Thee here in Thy holy Temple, and we pray Thee go forth with us, that in all we think, or do, or say, we may live ever as in Thy sign and service, through Jesus Christ our Lord. Amen.[1]

Many years ago, a visiting choir was singing at the outdoor Eucharist at St. Ann's Church in Kennebunkport, Maine. It was black-fly-season, and the guests were obviously uncomfortable. But a certain sacristan was prepared. With bug repellant in hand, former First Lady Barbara Bush, a long-time member of the Altar Guild in her home parish, moved quickly to spray the choir director and choristers. Right there, she demonstrated hospitality, concern for others, and thoroughness—all excellent virtues for an Altar Guild member.

I have attempted here to delve into the liturgical, theological, and historical ideas that underpin the worship life of the Church in an effort to set within a larger context the role of the Altar Guild. We have explored the rich tradition behind today's Altar Guild, and we have seen how their work is not just a series of necessary mundane tasks, but rather a sacred ministry that is infused with deep theological, ecclesiological, and liturgical significance.

To my fellow Clergy. If for some reason you have made it this far in the book, or maybe you've just turned to the conclusion, I offer this: Whether it's the one person who is there every Saturday and Sunday, or the well-oiled group that can handle six liturgies on a weekend without complaint, or, most likely, something in between, be gracious and grateful and remember to say, "thank you." Care for this hard-working group. Listen and learn from your Altar Guild.

---

1. G.T.S. Sacristan's Manual. c.1920.

I find my biggest mistakes come when I am so focused on what I want that I miss how these leaders desire to help. Their questions are not interruptions. Be a teacher: you have a liturgical and theological vision: share it so our sacristans can live into their vocation to be custodians of the sacred with you.

To the Altar Guild: As stewards of the sacred, it would be easy to fall into the trap of being museum curators. Ours is a living God, and our parishes are, hopefully, a dynamic expression of our faith and a representation of the living Body of Christ on earth today. God is always at work in the world around us if we but look and listen. To say it another way: Things change. Be flexible; be curious; be prepared; be compassionate; be joyful.

I am grateful for the folks who helped make this project come together: for Professor James Farwell's recommendation to take on this task; for Roma Maitlall, my editor, who was encouraging and showed abundant patience; for the people of St. Paul's, Rochester, who allowed me time to work on this project; for Bishop Kara and her kind words of introduction; for my friends and colleagues who supported me and listened to lectures they didn't sign up for; for the past and present sacristans and chief sacristans of the General Theological Seminary, and all sacristans everywhere; and, mostly especially, for the members of the Altar Guilds in the congregations where I have served whose patience, devotion, and dedication I greatly admire.

One last story. I was seated quietly in a pew before the liturgy was to begin. Each time another worshipper arrived, the pews creaked a little, tired after holding up the faithful for nearly two centuries. The prayer book, well-worn, flopped open—mine had pages no longer held by the binding. The hymnal had some wear and tear, having been lovingly used to sing praise to God for decades. There was a Bible, not a new edition and, unsurprisingly, still sturdy. My thoughts wandered from prayerful concerns to heartfelt thanksgivings to my grocery shopping list.

From the sacristy, two Altar Guild members appeared and stood before the altar. They noticed that the veil on the vested chalice was crooked and the "stack" was slightly off-center. They fussed a bit, stepped back, fussed some more, and then reviewed their work. The quiet organ voluntary was just beginning. One double-checked the flowers one last time as the other rearranged some books that would be needed by the acolytes and Eucharistic ministers. The care, the love, the desire for precision they possessed were so obvious. A smile came across my face; it was heartwarming, and I felt cared for, at home even, ready to share Holy Communion and offer our worship to God.

Of course, it was all more crooked and off-center than before. And, yet, it was beautiful, it was sacred.

> Finish then Thy new creation,
> pure and spotless let us be;
> Let us see Thy great salvation
> perfectly restored in Thee:
> Changed from glory into glory,
> till in heaven we take our place,
> till we cast our crowns before Thee,
> lost in wonder, love, and praise.[2]

---

2. Wesley, Charles. "Love divine, all loves excelling." *The Hymnal 1982* (New York: Church Pension Fund, 1985), 657.

APPENDIX A

SAMPLE CHECKLISTS

A ny sacristy I have been in has a binder of instructions dedicated to the work of the Altar Guild in that church. Standardization would be impossible, and even inappropriate, as each congregation is a unique expression of the Body of Christ. Based on the Altar Guild manual of St. Paul's Church in Rochester, New York, what follows is a series of sample checklists that might be able to serve as a guide for your ministry. Here, I am reminded of the little signs that occasionally appear by cash registers in stores: *need a penny, take a penny; have a penny, leave a penny.*

SUNDAY EUCHARISTS

Saturday Preparation and Set-up

____ CHECK ORDO AND ALTAR GUILD CALENDARS FOR LITURGICAL COLORS
Conform the High Altar and chantry superfrontals and pulpit and lectern palls to the color of the day.

____ SACRISTY COUNTER
Before beginning the set-ups, clean sacristy counter and set out counter cover that remains in place until all silver is returned to the safe.

____ FLOWERS
Once flowers have arrived, please check water level as very often florists keep the water level low in transit. If the flowers have not arrived by 10:30 a.m. telephone the florist first and then the Altar Flower Coordinator.

____ 8:00AM CHANTRY SET-UP

Arrange and leave on sacristy counter the 8:00 a.m. service the following for the chantry:

- Arrange the Stack:
  - Small chalice covered with purificator
  - Place bowl paten with one medium priest wafer on chalice
  - Place one pall on top of paten
  - Cover with silk veil and burse of same color with additional purificator in burse
- Small silver cruets, filled, with wine on right (cruet with garnet) and water on left
- Square ciborium filled with wafers, capacity of 50
- Lavabo with lavabo towel

Prepare the chantry:

- Remove weekday cover from free-standing altar
- Place linen on credence table
- Place corporal on altar (flush with priest-side of fair linen, with cross closer to priest)

____ 10:15AM HIGH ALTAR SET-UP

Then arrange and leave on the sacristy counter cover the following for the 10:00 a.m. service for the High Altar:

Arrange the stack:

- Small chalice covered with purificator
- Place bowl paten with one medium priest wafer on chalice
- Place one pall on top of paten
- Cover with silk veil and burse of same color with additional purificator in burse

For the High Altar credence table:

- One extra bowl paten
- One large chalice, covered with a purificator
- One large silver cruet with garnet, 1/3 filled with wine
- One large silver cruet, 1/3 filled with water
- Lavabo with lavabo towel

Arrange for narthex oblation table:

- Large silver flagon partially filled with wine
- Round silver ciborium filled with 150 loose wafers

Prepare the Sanctuary:

- Remove weekday covers from free-standing altar
- Place linen on credence table
- Place corporal on altar (flush with priest-side of fair linen, with cross closer to priest)

Arrange and leave on the long counter for the 8:00 a.m. and 10:15 a.m. services the following:

- Altar book (or binder) on missal stand
- Two small silver offertory plates (for 8:00am)
- Four large silver offertory plates (for 10:15am)

___ OTHER TASKS

To be done each week:

- Check altar and office candles, replenish oil and clean as needed
- Sweep or vacuum sanctuary floors
- Brush or vacuum kneelers at chantry and sanctuary altar rails
- Check columbarium and replenish water levels of flowers and remove flower dead or withering blooms

To be done monthly:

- Week One: Change fair linens on all altars
- Week Two: Dust and polish wood in sanctuary
- Week Three: Dust and polish chantry
- Week Four: Dust and polish chapel and polish sanctuary gates

Sunday Set-up and Clean-up

___ 8:00AM CHANTRY SET-UP

Arrive 30 minutes early (7:30am) so you have time to accomplish your tasks with being rushed:

Place on chantry altar:

- Vested chalice on the corporal on the chantry altar
- Altar book and stand to priest's left on the altar

Place on credence table:

- Small silver cruets, filled, with wine on right (cruet with garnet) and water on left
- Square ciborium filled with wafers, capacity of 50
- Lavabo with lavabo towel

Set-Out

- Small silver offertory plates

Following the service:

- Remove all Eucharistic vessels to sacristy
- Carefully pour consecrated wine in chalice into piscina, rinse with water and pour down piscina
- Clean and replace in safe all silver
- Place offerings in safe in bag marked "8:00am Offering"

___ 10:15AM SANCTUARY SET-UP

Place on sanctuary altar:

- Vested chalice on the corporal on the sanctuary altar
- Altar book and stand to priest's left on the altar

Place on credence table:

- One extra bowl paten
- One large chalice, covered with a purificator
- One large silver cruet with garnet, 1/3 filled with wine
- One large silver cruet, 1/3 filled with water
- Lavabo with lavabo towel

Arrange narthex oblation table:

- Offering plates
- Large silver flagon partially filled with wine
- Round silver ciborium

Following the service:

- Remove all Eucharistic vessels to sacristy
- Carefully pour consecrated wine in chalice into piscina, rinse with water and pour down piscina
- Clean and replace in safe all silver
- Place offerings in safe in bag marked "10:15am Offering"
- Returning silks to drawers
- Rinse soiled linens and leave them hanging on the cupboard towel racks.
- Remove corporals from all altars
- Remove covers from credence tables
- Replace weekday covers over fair linens on all altars

WEEKDAY EUCHARIST

Arrive 45 minutes early (11:15am) so you have time to accomplish your tasks without being rushed:

Prepare the chapel:

- Check Ordo calendar and conform the superfrontal to the color of the day.
- Remove weekday cover from altar
- Place linen on credence table
- Place corporal on altar (flush with priest-side of fair linen, with cross closer to priest)

Arrange the stack:

- Small chalice covered with purificator
- Place bowl paten with one medium priest wafer on chalice
- Place one pall on top of paten
- Cover with silk veil and burse of same color with additional purificator in burse

Place on chapel altar:

- Vested chalice on the corporal on the chantry altar
- Altar book and stand to priest's left on the altar

Place on credence shelf:

- Small silver cruets, filled, with wine on right (cruet with garnet) and water on left
- Square ciborium filled with wafers, capacity of 50
- Lavabo with lavabo towel

Additional tasks:

- Put out small wooden offertory plate
- Light altar candles (at 11:50am)

Following the service:

- Remove all Eucharistic vessels to sacristy
- Extinguish candles
- Carefully pour consecrated wine in chalice into piscina, rinse with water and pour down piscina
- Clean and replace in safe all silver
- Place any offerings in safe in bag "offerings"
- Rinse soiled linens and leave them hanging on the cupboard towel racks.
- Remove corporal from chapel altar
- Remove covers from credence shelves
- Replace weekday covers over fair linens on altar

OUTDOOR EUCHARIST

Arrive 45 minutes early (4:45pm) so you have time to accomplish your tasks without being rushed:

Arrange the stack:

- Clay chalice covered with purificator
- Place clay paten with one large priest wafer on chalice
- Place one pall on top of paten

Prepare the altar:

- Clean altar, as needed
- Place corporal on altar (flush with priest-side of fair linen, with cross closer to priest); use the glass "weights" to hold it in place
- Place "stack" on the corporal on the altar
- Altar book to priest's left on the altar

Place on altar (but not on corporal):

- Small glass cruets, filled, with wine and water

Additional tasks:

- Put out baskets with bulletins and readings
- Put out basket for offerings

Following the service:

- Remove all Eucharistic vessels and linens to sacristy
- Carefully pour consecrated wine in chalice into piscina, rinse with water and pour down piscina
- Clean and replace all Eucharistic vessels
- Rinse linens and hang on drying rack
- Place any offerings in safe in bag "offerings"

SPECIAL SERVICES

Baptisms

The Sexton will place the baptismal font at the top of the chancel steps, the Paschal candle on its stand near the font, and a small table behind the font in the chancel for your use.

The Altar Guild will place the following on the small table:

- Table linen
- Ewer partially filled with *warm* water
- Baptismal shell (for pouring water)
- Baptismal towel (for each person)
- Baptismal candle (for each person)
- Silver stock of chrism (from High Altar aumbry)
- Baptismal gift in white box (for each person)

Weddings

- Color of the day is white: Ensure all frontals and hangings conform

- The white High Altar kneeling cushion is used at the High Altar rail
- Coordinate with wedding verger and officiant if additional help is needed
- Set-up for Eucharist, if needed
- Following the service return the hangings to the current color.

Funerals

- Color of the day is white: Ensure all frontals and hangings conform
- Funerals may have either a casket or an urn.
  - If a casket, it is covered with a funeral pall which is to be placed in the narthex.
  - If an urn, the sexton will place a small table in the chancel that is to be covered with linen before setting the urn into position. The urn is covered with a white silk veil.
- The Paschal candle will be lit.
- Coordinate with officiant if additional help is needed
- Set-up for Eucharist, if needed
- Following the service return the hangings to the current color.

Daily Office

- Ensure all frontals and hangings conform to color of day
- Light office candles
- Coordinate with officiant if additional help is needed

SEASONAL CHECKLISTS

Again, details will vary from congregation to congregation around customs for each of these seasons and feast days. What follows are suggestions for the Altar Guild to keep at top of mind as you prepare.

Remember good, clear communication with the clergy and other leaders is crucial.

ADVENT

One month before Advent begins

- Ensure that you have the appropriate candles for the Advent wreath
- Confirm with the clergy what additional services might occur and what roles, if any, the Altar Guild will need to play
- Confirm antependium and vestments are clean and in good condition
- Plan any special decorations

At the beginning of and during Advent

- Confirm your schedules and checklists
- Meet with the clergy to discuss Christmas

At the end of Advent

- Debrief the season and make notes for the next year, if needed
- Ensure the antependium and vestments are in good order and clean
- Return Advent wreath and candles to storage, if necessary

CHRISTMAS

One month before Christmas

- Meet with clergy and other leaders to discuss Christmas liturgies. Good questions to ask might be:
  - How many Christmas Eve / Day liturgies are there?
  - Is there anything special we should know about?

- ○ Will extra candles be used?
- ○ What other special services might be taking place and does the Altar Guild need to help?
- Confirm antependium and vestments are clean and in good condition
- Clean vestments (i.e. acolyte albs, clergy vestments, etc.), as needed
- Plan any special decorations and set Christmas decorating dates

After Christmas

- Debrief and make notes for the next year, if needed: *what worked well, what needs attention, any suggestions*
- Ensure the antependium and vestments are in good order and clean

LENT

One month before Ash Wednesday

- Meet with clergy and other leaders to discuss Ash Wednesday and other Lenten liturgies
- Do you have ashes? Will you order or will they be "made" from the prior year's old palms from Palm Sunday?
- Confirm antependium and vestments are clean and in good condition

Days leading up to Ash Wednesday

- Confirm your schedules and checklists
- Veil crosses and statues, if that is your custom
- Ensure you have appropriate means for cleaning ashes from fingers and hands. [The custom has been lemons and stale bread. More symbolic than effective.]

During Lent

- Assign extra "spring cleaning" tasks to Altar Guild teams:
  - Week One: Conduct inventory of vestments and vessels (I)
  - Week Two: Conduct inventory of vestments and vessels (II)
  - Week Three: Thoroughly clean sacristy
  - Week Four: Clean and prepare vestments
  - Week Five: Polish rarely used brass and silver vessels

After Lent

- Debrief and make notes for the next year, if needed: *likes, concerns, wishes*
- Ensure the antependium and vestments are in good order and clean

Holy Week

One month before Palm Sunday

- Meet with clergy and other leaders to discuss Holy Week liturgies and create details checklists. Good questions to ask:
  - Is there a daily Eucharist?
  - Is there a foot-washing on Maundy Thursday? How do you envision that happening?
  - How will the stripping of the altar take place on Maundy Thursday?
  - Is there Communion on Good Friday? What do you need?
- Order palms
- Confirm antependium and vestments are clean and in good condition

Days before Palm Sunday

- Confirm your schedules and checklists for Holy Week
- Confirm where / how palms will be distributed

- Change antependium for conform with liturgical color
- Change veils on crosses and statues, if that is your custom

After Holy Week

- Debrief and make notes for the next year, if needed: *likes, concerns, wishes*
- Ensure the antependium and vestments are in good order and clean
- Easter and day of Pentecost

One month before Easter

- Meet with clergy and other leaders to discuss Easter liturgies and create details checklists. Good questions to ask:
  - Is there a Great Vigil of Easter? What is the set-up?
  - How many Easter Day liturgies are there?
  - Are there any customs you'd like us to be aware of?
  - What other special services might happen during the year?
  - Anything special for Pentecost?
- Plan special decorations and set time for decorating on Holy Saturday

Holy Saturday: The great decorating for Easter

- Change antependium for conform with liturgical color
- Remove veils from crosses and statues, if that is your custom
- Re-set linens
- Polish silver and brass
- Replace / re-fill candles
- Decorate—being mindful not to distract from the purposes liturgical spaces and centers (see chapter four)
- Put new Holy Oils, if available, in Aumbry
- Ask the clergy—who better be there with you!—what else they need

After Easter

- Debrief and make notes for the next year, if needed: *likes, concerns, wishes*
- Ensure the antependium and vestments are in good order and clean

SEASON AFTER PENTECOST / ORDINARY TIME

A few weeks before Trinity Sunday:

- Meet with clergy and other leaders to discuss what's the upcoming calendar looks like.
- Ensure antependium and vestments are clean and in good condition

During the "Long Green Season:"

- Meet again with clergy and other leaders to discuss what's the upcoming calendar looks like and what the Altar Guild might need to do. A few questions to ask:
  - Are we doing anything special for Rally Day?
  - What are we doing for All Saints' Sunday?
  - What are the plans for Thanksgiving?
- Ensure the antependium and vestments remain in good order and clean
- Get special projects done
- Make notes for the next year, if needed: *what worked well, what needs attention, any suggestions*

APPENDIX B

ILLUSTRATIONS

From the St. Paul's Church, Rochester, Altar Guild Manual
Illustrations by Sonja Slother

1. As we saw in our discussion on the Eucharist, the Book of Common Prayer presumes the preparing of the altar at the offertory. Given this, the vested chalice ("the stack") would best be placed on the credence table from the beginning of the service.

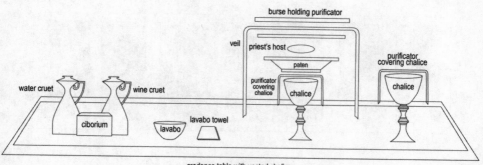

credence table with vested chalice

2. In some cases, especially when space is limited, it is the custom
   to place the veiled chalice on the altar in advance with the
   bread and wine being placed at the offertory. Facing a free-
   standing altar, this would be the view.

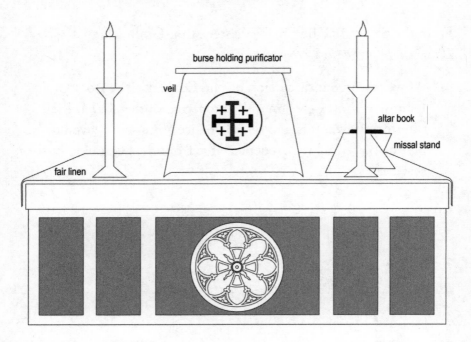

3. A view of "the stack" standing behind the altar and facing the congregation.

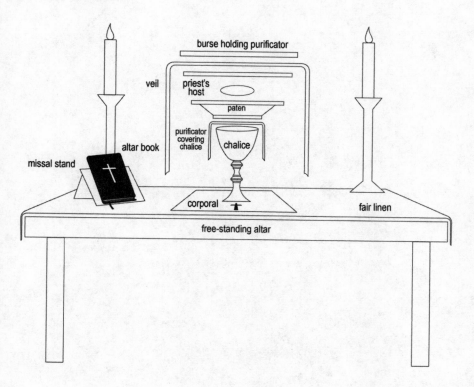

4. A sample set-up for the credence table without the vested chalice.

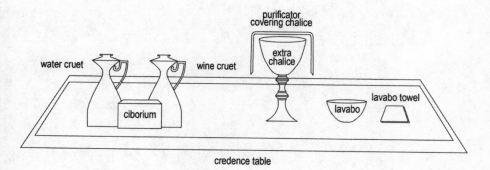

APPENDIX C

SAMPLE SCHEDULE

Weekly schedules, monthly schedules, assigned dates, sign-up for dates, etc.: there are plenty of ways to manage the rotation of members. Each Altar Guild must figure out what works best for their parish and the individual sacristans—and regular reevaluation of the practice is important. A weekly rotation of members would seem to work best with each team covering all liturgies (e.g. funerals, weddings, etc.) that week. However, with changing demographics, employment schedules, smaller churches, and fewer members, flexibility is always key. What follows is a sample weekly schedule that runs from Saturday to Saturday. While it may be helpful, it may also be unrealistic; use it as you wish.

TEAM MATTHEW
G. Worde, Lead; E. Ahearn; I. Middlebury
November 30 (Advent 1)
December 21—All Teams (Christmas)
December 28
January 25
February 22
March 22
April 12—All Teams (Holy Week)
April 19—All Teams (Easter) **
April 26
May 17

TEAM MARK
K. Stohl, Lead; S. Paulson; J. Kevens
December 7
December 21—All Teams (Christmas)

January 4
February 1
March 1 (Ash Wednesday)
March 29*
April 12—All Teams (Holy Week)
April 19—All Teams (Easter)
April 26
May 24

TEAM LUKE
P. Canton, Lead; L. Mack; A. Wagner
December 14
December 21—All Teams (Christmas)
January 11
February 8
March 8*
April 5
April 12—All Teams (Holy Week)
April 19—All Teams (Easter)
May 3
May 31

TEAM JOHN
S. Connors, Lead; J. Steves; H. Lyon
December 21—All Teams (Christmas)**
January 18
February 15
March 15*
April 12—All Teams (Holy Week)**
April 19—All Teams (Easter)
May 10
June 7

*Special Lenten assignment
**Primary team with assistance from other members

SELECTED ARTICLES

From the National Altar Guild Association
https://nationalaltarguildassociation.org/

STITCHES IN TIME

by Sharon Sheridan for *Episcopal Life*

Vestments and altar hangings are more than a colorful, occasionally changing backdrop to worship. They are congregational treasurers that enhance the liturgy, says Mary Wagner, who volunteers in preserving and repairing vestments at the Convent of St. John Baptist in Mendham, N.J.

"The vestments—whatever they are, they could be simple canvas; they don't have to be elaborate—they are the treasures of your church, and through them is another way of holding your attention when you are in the house of God," she says. Whether burlap or brocade, they're "invaluable as far as I'm concerned."

Wagner works to preserve such treasures, and teach others how to do it. In February, she and fellow convent volunteer and ecclesiastical embroiderer Carol Homer will lead a workshop on vestment restoration in Mendham.

The art of vestment repair and preservation isn't as tricky as some fear, Homer notes.

"I am convinced that in every congregation you have the talent to save and preserve these things," she says. "Sometimes it's a simple stitch or a matter of housecleaning—I don't really expect to make people expert stitchers. I think that a lot of people are capable of doing it. Are they going to do an absolute expert job? Probably not. But you probably don't need an absolute expert job."

"Good housekeeping does a lot." Examine vestment storage areas. Are there leaks or "creepy crawlies" such as mice or insects? Is the room excessively hot in summer or unheated in winter?

"Look for moisture. If you have metal handles—and they're getting rusty, that's a bad sign." You may want to install a dehumidifier.

Don't just eyeball a full storage area. "You have to take everything out, one by one—It's a good idea to take things out once a year and just let them breathe."

Hang vestments on fabric-padded hangers. Wire hangers eventually cut the fabric, damaging the shoulder areas, "which can be costly to repair." The hangers should be unwrinkled at the top, where garments will touch, and stitched on the bottom, so that the garment won't rub against the stitching.

Store hanging vestments beneath a simple muslin or cotton cover, stitched down the front.

Line wood storage drawers with Tyvek, a durable substance that protects vestments from dust and prevents stains from the wood.

Don't wear jewelry such as rings while handling vestments.

To clean an old, dusty vestment, try vacuuming it. Wrap the vacuum nozzle six to eight times with old pantyhose, then secure it with an elastic band. Place a screen over the garment. Vacuum on the lowest setting, cleaning the inside of the garment first. Work in a pattern—for example, top to bottom—to be sure to get every inch. When cleaning the outside, double or triple the screen and barely touch it with the nozzle when vacuuming over stitching. "You will find a marked difference in the garment if you have the patience and the time to do this. It's a very delicate operation. I prefer that people do it in front of me the first time."

Catalogue your collection. Photograph vestments front and back, on a person and hanging alone. Make two copies and place each with an identical notebook listing the vestments. If you wish, add details about the history of each vestment, such as when it was dedicated.

You also can include photographs of how the altar is set up for various occasions, such as Easter.

Keep one copy of the catalogue at the church, the other stored safely offsite. It will prove invaluable in case of fire. Photos also provide a convenient way to show someone your vestments. "You don't have to drag them through your collection."

CLEAN, PROTECT AND STORE YOUR SILVER

How to Recognize Silver

Sterling silver is 92.5% silver and 7.5% copper. In the U.S.A. sterling silver will be stamped "sterling." Mexican silver is stamped 92.5. English sterling is stamped with a lion facing to the left.

Silver plate consists of a base metal (often copper) that has been electrolytically coated with silver. In the U.S.A. it will be stamped plate. In England it will be stamped with a lion facing to the right.

Handling and Storing Silver

This is the best way to preserve your silver and if done faithfully will require little or no polishing for long periods of time:

- Use cotton or plastic gloves.
- Wash your silver in mild non-lemon-scented phosphate-free detergent as soon as you are finished using it.
- Dry thoroughly with a soft cotton towel (for intricate detail use a cotton Q-tip to get into cracks and crevices).
- Store wrapped in acid-free tissue and in a sealed polyethylene bag (e.g., Ziploc) or in a Pacific Silvercloth bag (don't get the Pacific cloth wet as it will remove the tarnish deterrent properties).

Things that can Damage Silver and Cause Tarnish

All sulfur-containing compounds:

- Air pollutants from fossil fuels
- Textiles containing wool, felt and velvet
- Rubber products, such as foam rubber, carpet padding and rubber bands
- Wood (untreated), paper and cardboard
- Foods such as olive oil, vinegar, olives, pickled products, eggs and egg products
- Oils and salts from your hands
- Wine and fruit juice (gold-lined chalices combat corrosion)
- Salt is very corrosive
- Humidity hastens tarnish

To Remove Tarnish

First, thoroughly wash and dry your silver as noted.

For lightly tarnished silver buy a good nonabrasive polish such as Blitz (found at Amazon.com) or WOW (a product from Almy that works great). To test a polish for abrasiveness, rub it between your fingers. It should feel like talcum powder. If it feels gritty at all do not use it.

Heavy tarnish may be removed with Tarnex, but it is not recommended as it may leave a yellow cast on the silver, dulling it over time. It also has no tarnish prevention properties and may pit.

Polish with an old terry cloth towel and a wet Q-tip, a soft wet tampico or horsehair brush to remove the polish from intricate detail. Buff with a soft cotton cloth.

A Few Don'ts

- Don't put your silver in the dishwasher—the heat and harsh detergent may cause damage.

- Don't wrap silver in saran wrap or plastic cleaning bags. Both will stick and cause permanent yellowing.
- Never use rubber bands on silver. They will cause permanent damage.
- Don't wrap in newspaper as it will leave print on the silver and ultimately tarnish.
- Don't use silver polish that has dried out as it will be too concentrated with abrasives.
- Do not store weighted hollowware in hot attics, or place in ovens or dishwashers as these will cause damage.
- Don't polish gold, which does not tarnish. Polish will eventually rub the gold down to the base metal.
- To protect lacquered brass always handle with gloves. Make sure an alcohol-free hand sanitizer is used by those touching the brass during a service. If there is some pitting of the lacquer, lightly rub a wooden match in the pit to get rid of it. Olive oil may be used to clean and bring out the luster.

A good silver website

http://www.silversmithing.com/care.htm

STEWARDSHIP OF LINENS
by JoAnn Ziller

One of the most comprehensive and informative workshops held at [the Triennial gathering of the National Altar Guild Association in 2012] in Indianapolis was conducted by Alice Scarbrough from the Diocese of Texas. All aspects of linen construction and maintenance were covered. Alice emphasized that this meant stewardship—constructing, taking care and extending the life of our linens was another form of stewardship within our worship experience. If you have a chance to participate in a workshop held by Alice, I highly recommend that you do so. Her amazingly wide range of knowledge concerning altar linens is not to be missed. Workshops such as this show us why attending future Triennial NAGA meetings has great value.

Here are a few invaluable tips from the workshop.

Alice's Stain Removal Tips

- It is important to remove any stain as soon as possible.
- Grease stains—It is best to use a dry process.
  - Use talcum powder, pharmaceutical talc, white tailor's chalk, or Fuller's Earth
  - Use white blotting paper, place paper down first, sprinkle with powder, put fabric next powder, next sprinkle the fabric with a small amount of powder and top with white blotting paper. Let this stand for several hours, then iron. Wash after this process.
- Wine and fruit stains—Rub the stain with ice cubes and blot as quickly as possible.
  - Spot clean with Orvus and distilled water solution, then the wash item.
  - Rub the stain with a damp piece of Ivory soap and allow to stand for several hours. Rinse well and wash.
  - Rinse a red wine stain with white wine.
- Tea and coffee stains—Wash in soap and water or use Shout, Oxiclean, or Arm & Hammer
- Ink—Soak the stain in warm milk or lemon juice and salt.
- Wax—Iron with fabric sandwiched between two layers of white blotting paper.
- Blood—Use the saliva from the person who's blood it is or use dog's saliva. Another person's salvia will not work.

- Stubborn stains (age spots and rust)—Soak in solution of white toothpaste and distilled water. Rub in with a soft brush. Allow to dry and rinse. Reapply if needed. Some stains need many applications to work.
- Lipstick—Use the grease process or use Zout.
- Clorox—Do not use. This breaks down and weakens the fibers in the fabric.

General Laundry

- White linens—Hand wash in cool or room temperature water using a mild soap (Ivory or lanolin). If heavily soiled use Orvus or OxiClean and distilled water.
- Silk—Dry clean or use vinegar and distilled water. If using vinegar and distilled water, test for color fasting first.
- Rinsing—If white vinegar is added to the rinse water it will give sheen to the embroidery.
- Drying—flat dry whenever possible. Hang item if it is too large. Do not put in dryer because of heat.
- Starching—Do not starch ecclesiastical items
- Ironing—Iron from the center out, upside down, being careful around the corners of embroidery. Do not steam in order to avoid rust spots. Use a covered plywood board for the ironing of fair linens. Iron as little as possible in order to extend the life of our linens.

ADVENT FLOWER NOTES

by Linda Roeckelein

For me the most joyous years are those when Advent I is the Sunday after Thanksgiving weekend. At Washington National Cathedral, our Thanksgiving arrangements are bountiful, filled with glorious fruits and blossoms and branches that we have dried or preserved in glycerin. The Cathedral is visited by hundreds of visitors, many interested in seeing our displays and sharing their ideas.

This year, like so many others before, on Friday and Saturday after turkey dinners and turkey soup, we will dismantle all of the golds and oranges and reds, replacing them with evergreens, ivy and magnolia. Our Canterbury pulpit and lectern will be hung with green garlands.

During the course of Advent, all altars will be decorated with a mixture of greenery. I call it a "green salad" when our volunteers come in to choose the cedar, juniper, balsam, pine, and other treasures from the buffet of assorted greens they will use in their arrangements. Though we are still aglow from our family gatherings, there is an amazing comfort and elegance in the scent and simplicity of the Advent greens. Like age we soon learn to respect and accept these displays even when they become rather crisp!

This year at the Cathedral, we are breaking tradition. Our Dean and Canon Precentor would like some Christmas color for Advent IV. Therefore for that Sunday we will bring out some of the 500 individual potted poinsettias we have put into quart-size plastic bags, some wide-wired red ribbon, crab, lady and Rome apples, cones, and nandina berries. Our services will be filled with joyous Christmas music and we will start celebrating the magic of Christmas a bit earlier than usual. During the next few days we will be adding hydrangeas, gold-enhanced greenery, carnations (for which we must all be thankful), winterberries, ginger, and preserved roses.

I must choose material carefully for all to last until Epiphany. Our designs vary from year to year. I think the one photographed here, for our High Altar, is the most beautiful we have done in my 43 years on the guild. Credit goes to Tania Palmer who carefully attached each poinsettia to a garden arch.

I wish you all the joys of Christmas as you decorate your churches aware of God's kindness in the beauty of flowers.

3 Christmas Decorating Tips:

To bag poinsettias: use individual 4½ inch poinsettia plants. First day water thoroughly. Second day, tip out of the pot and with soil, slip each plant into a quart-size plastic bag. If this is a Ziploc, cut off the "zip." Close the bag tightly around the stem with ½ a chenille stem (pipe cleaner).

Shellac all fruit with "bull's eye" shellac. Apples will last longer and beautifully reflect the light.

The preserved roses we use come from Mirsky, Inc. or Mountain Farms, Inc. If you intend to use these roses in arrangements and wish to use them again as we do, you will need to wire them; otherwise, they can be glued in place on a wreath or topiary.

THE COLORS OF CHRISTMAS
by Michael Kobel and Keith Shaw, Principals, MKBuds,
San Mateo, CA

Special seasonal interest on the altar helps to unite the time of year with the many church celebrations of the Episcopal Church year. Advent, Christmas, Epiphany, Easter, the Feasts, as well as winter, summer, fall and spring are all important to consider when designing the altar flowers. At this time of year, we focus on floral design for Advent through Christmas.

In the winter, especially during the weeks of Advent, we see lots of red berries, variegated and green hollies, winterberry, evergreen boughs, ivies, white and gray birch twigs and sticks, white lilies, hydrangeas, white calla lilies, red and/or white roses, white and/or pink amaryllis. When choosing flowers, consider the colors you'd like to display.

For those who enjoy the traditional colors of the season, nothing is more festive than a red, green and white palette during Advent through Christmas Eve. On Christmas Day think about changing the colors to all white flowers with evergreen boughs and birch stems. You could even put a bit of silver gray into the mix.

For those Episcopal churches that use light or darker blue as the color of the Advent season, choose a color palette of white, off-white, pale beige and light blue. Obviously use no red, gold or bright yellow. You could use white lilies, white French tulips and white spider mums sprayed with a light blue dusting to pick up the color of the altar paraments. Then you might use traditional variegated greens, white birch stems and some very pale yellows as a subtle accent to pick up the brass altar vases and vessels. This combination of colors is very effective and integrates the colors used throughout the church—from the altar to the baptismal font.

Consider, too, the maintenance of your floral arrangements as you may need to refresh the flowers throughout the week for special seasonal services. One way to keep flowers fresh is to put a jigger of inexpensive vodka in the vase water. Not only does this help to keep the water clean, but it also helps the stems stay open to drink and absorb the water. If you use white or red poinsettias in your vases, take a candle flame (or lighter) and sear the end of the cut stem. This stops the poinsettia from wilting and prevents the stem sap from interfering with other flowers in the arrangement.

If you like to include Christmas trees in your design, you might think about decorating them with white or blue lights. However, the aesthetics can be quite effective when they are left unadorned; that is, no ornamentation with the exception of tall white birch stems bundled and placed at the top of the tree to create a starburst effect. This is a very beautiful way to reflect a natural feeling but with a bit of baroque majesty suiting the season. Three fir trees of different sizes grouped together either at the back of the church around the font and/or on the side of the main altar (if there is room) is another elegant possibility. Surround the base of the tree (or trees) with white poinsettias. This simple arrangement lasts all season and allows the evergreen freshness to filter throughout the church.

Don't forget about window arrangements. Use the same flowers, color palette and materials to integrate themes. Make sure that all your arrangements and trees are kept well watered. Use the vodka for horticultural reasons (well, maybe a shot for you, too?).

Now step back and enjoy the season. Merry Christmas!

EPIPHANY FLOWER NOTES
by Clara Fowler

Epiphany comes so soon after Christmas that often your greens and plants are still in usable condition. The Epiphany Sunday does often ask for the star colors of white and gold, so in my arrangements for that day, I reach out with those colors like rays.

After all the red of Christmas, it is a nice change. The season can be long or short and any color goes since the liturgical one is green. A good budget will allow the purchase of flowers. Small budgets will send you to the big box stores and large groceries. You may be able to use some of your poinsettias. Don't forget houseplants: some ferns, sanserveria, ivy, and aspidistra grown in a pot will allow you some cutting.

One small church where we belonged had two lovely brass boxes with small philodendron on trellises. The plants spent the week in a sunny sacristy and were pruned, watered and very well cared for to look great on a white wall. We also had two gorgeous dry arrangements that we stored in large vases. We dressed these up for Sundays with a few bright flowers in water picks.

Epiphany and Lent are two good seasons to train new members for the flower guild and have workshops to remind the guild members of the basics we forget like: clean all containers, no leaves under water, cut off—do not pull out dead things, run the broad side of the oasis on the side of a round vase, leave watering room, and CLEAN UP. Doing flowers is the most fun of the Altar Guild ministries.

HOLY WEEK, EASTER, SPRING FLOWERS
by Clara Fowler

Holy Week opens with Palm Sunday and we arrange with a variety of palms, if we are fortunate. Some ferns: jade, leather leaf and Boston will look like a palm and lighten the arrangement. If you clip off ragged edges of palms with regular scissors and arrange palms as they grow, they act better. The Bible says branches, so many churches today add flowering spring branches. I also add the palm pieces the people receive—straight or bent to add light to the arrangement. Many Orthodox churches add pussy willow branches to the palms, which also add light.

Maundy Thursday for some churches means a floral offering in which to place the reserved sacrament. Then a bare Friday and Saturday, until the eager flower guild comes.

Easter gives us the opportunity to arrange everywhere and the spring flowers are so beautiful. Lilies are traditional, but many churches use other flowers as well. Colors other than white and yellow are seen on altars and in windows. Do you decorate the Paschal candle? Many have a circle on the holder to use. If not, there are many products on the market that are safe to use (oasis makes it easy to use small holders you can encircle the candlestick with). Some guilds do arrangements on the font. It may be in use so either leave a space in a wreath or do a garden below. Window and door arrangements are fun to do.

It's also an opportunity to use outside helpers and interest others in the guild. Many Altar Guilds including mine place lily plants around the church, the font area and the chancel. In my parish this year we may use hydrangeas, roses and other flowering plants as well. We arrange with spring colors. In the picture the palms have been reused from Palm Sunday.

Beware of lily pollen on material. It should be blown off, removed with a soft brush or a chenille stick. Do not rub it! If it does stain, pretreat it as a protein. There are good laundry products for this.

Avoid bleach on linen or easy care. The whole pollen problem can be avoided by removing the pollen sacs when the lily first opens and before the pollen matures.

FALL FLOWER NOTES
by Clara Fowler

Summer ends and the majority of the flowers fade. Now is the time to collect seedpods, grasses with plumes and leaves.

Drying Flowers for Fall Arrangement

Cut branches and remove the lower leaves. To preserve, stand them in a jar containing two-three inches of glycerin and water, mixed two parts water and one part glycerin, or in straight antifreeze. Place them in a light, cool room away from animals and children. When the leaves change color and are pliable with a slight oily feel, they are done. Check every day. Over-done stems mildew easily. Lay the branches in a box to dry the stem end. To store the branches, either stand them in a container in a dry area or place them in a newspaper-lined box. Branches can be refreshed using steam or wiped with soapy water and then rinsed and dried well. They may be painted or pressed using a cool iron. Use Sahara (dry foam) for dry arranging.

A few other fall hints:

- Spray fuzzy seed heads with hair spray or fixative to prevent shedding.
- A few spots of bright color like red or orange help dried arrangements. Use flower tubes and put in some bright carnations or gerberas.
- If fruit or vegetables are to remain long on the altar, brush shellac on them to halt any deterioration. Bananas should not be used for more than one day. Do not use real grapes. (They

fall off the stem.) If the product is to be used one day and can be cooked afterward, use bamboo skewers to put them into the foam.

Graceful Vase Arrangements

For the traditional altars and chapels that are still using vases, here are several suggestions for making graceful arrangements:

If you use Oasis, always use standard or advantage. It takes a little longer to soak, but it does not crumble as fast. It should stick about two inches above the rim of the vase. Oasis is shaped like a brick with wide sides and narrow ends. When placed in the vase have the wider dimension along the sides. (The narrow edge will be facing you.) This allows full use of the sides of the brick.

Placing greens and flowers so that they drop below the rim of the vase makes a pleasing look.

If using a small-necked vase, you might put a small green designer bowl from your florist on top of the vase. It can be stuck down with sticky clay but the weight will hold it.

A round plywood platform painted dark green with a dowel that goes down into the vase might also be used.

Many of these church vases are very old and must be treated with respect, but we should use them.

TIPS FOR RECRUITING ALTAR GUILD MEMBERS

The recruitment and retention of new Altar Guild members is always a challenge. We are pleased to offer some suggestions, thanks to Province VII, that may prove helpful.

- **Be Welcoming**: Welcome everyone who shows an interest, including men. This should go without saying, but unfortunately is not always the case. "Demystify" the Altar Guild and its work.

- **New Member Packets**: Include information on Altar Guild membership in the new member packets distributed by your parish.

- **Weekly Service Bulletins**: List the Altar Guild members on duty that week in your weekly service bulletins.

- **Personal Contact**: Recruit in person. Don't just rely on bulletins or newsletter notices. Remember, people need to be needed.

- **Utilize Particular Skills**: Is there someone who likes to polish silver/brass? Someone who enjoys decorating? Ask her/him to come in only when that activity is going on. Once they get to know you and see what else goes on, they may sign on for regular duty. Until then, there's extra help.

- **Encourage New Ideas**: "We've always done it that way," is merely a statement of fact. Why search for new, younger members and then fail to take advantage of their ideas?

- **Trial Periods for New Members**: Like anything else, Altar Guild service is not for everyone. Invite new people to a meeting, schedule them for two or three months before asking them to make a commitment.

- **Prayerfulness and Liturgical Knowledge**: Altar Guild ministry is first and foremost a ministry of prayerfulness. Emphasize the liturgical knowledge that comes from Altar Guild service. Don't let the busyness get in the way.

- **Keep It Simple for New Members**: Utilize checklists, post photographs or diagrams of sacristy and altar setups, and provide individual manuals. (This helps the older and forgetful, too!)

- **Flexible Scheduling**: Allow for flexible schedules. New members might be more apt to join if schedules are more accommodating.

- **Family Service**: Consider inviting families to join. Ask a different family to sign up to provide Altar Guild service each week of the calendar year.
- **Promote the Altar Guild (just a little)**: Have a yearly installation ceremony at the main service so that the congregation can see who's on the Altar Guild. Have each Altar Guild member wear an Altar Guild pin when on duty.
- **Be Positive**: We tend to grumble about our ministry even though most of us love it dearly. Think about how it sounds to nonmembers. Spread the Altar Guild spirit. Think about placing a sign on the sacristy door that reads, "Kindness spoken here."

ALTAR GUILD...THE NEXT GENERATION
by Deborah Bradley

At our meeting in Salt Lake City, a question arose on how to attract new members to the Altar Guild. I had the pleasure of sharing how our little parish in Texas was able to foster an interest and gain new team members by inviting the children to help us. Later, several asked me "What exactly did you do?" So, I thought perhaps I would take this opportunity to share in finer detail how we did it...

I think it important to mention that St. James is a very small church, with a congregation of mainly retirees. We never have more than a handful of kids. However, as with most, Easter is a time when our churches are full to capacity. Many visitors and newcomers, many with kids, come from far and near to share the blessings of this day. At that time, I was a mother of young ones. So, I seized the opportunity to make sure all of the children knew how important they were in the celebration of Easter. I invited parents and kids alike, to help us "Set HIS Table" for that morning's late service. It didn't take any longer than usual and it was great fun to have so many "helpers" buzzing about making sure that our Festival Eucharist was a true Parish family celebration.

They learned technical terms like ciborium and cruet. They helped our altar team count the communion wafers, fold purificators and "wash the dishes." Even now, I am moved at the memory of their little faces as they began to truly understand what the bread and wine really meant. It was touching how the older ones would govern the younger ones, making sure there were no "Sacristy shenanigans." They were all so eager to help in preparing for that special time in our Sunday service, and the moms enjoyed watching their kids explore and discover something that was otherwise a mystery to them.

When we were finished, each child received a small prize from a treasure chest that reflected a celebratory Easter message. They also were given a little sticker that read "I set HIS table today!" I remember one little guy in particular, Luke. He was four years old and the sticker almost covered his whole chest. He wore that sticker during the service, all through the Easter egg hunt and playground time. His mom reported that he carefully placed the sticker on his pajamas that night and planned to wear it every day, until the next Sunday—when he could set Jesus' table again!

From that moment on, there was a renewed spirit in our Altar Guild. (Yep, that was truly what we had hoped for.) That wonderful little experiment gained our Altar Guild two new team members: one was a mom and the other was someone that was excited about what we had done with the kids.

Now, we take great care to invite the kids and their families to help with other duties like "the Big Clean," making Palm Crosses and Advent Wreathes, Rally Day, decorating for Christmas and just about any other opportunity we can think of.

All of those kids are now grown and serve as acolytes, readers, choir members and, yes, even help on the Altar Guild. Every once in a while, one of them will recall that first Easter service and how "cool" it was to be a part of something so BIG. That impression on their hearts shows me, and our entire parish family, that the future of our church is in good hands.

So, to answer your question...embrace the talents and freshness that the young (and youngish) may provide. You might be surprised at the way your Altar Guild may grow. Be blessed!

APPENDIX E
ADDITIONAL RESOURCES

Without counsel, plans go wrong,
but with many advisers they succeed.

(Proverbs 15:22)

An outstanding go-to online resource:

National Altar Guild Association
https://nationalaltarguildassociation.org/

Recommended Books for your Sacristy

Book of Common Prayer, 1979
Enriching our Worship, vols. 1-6
Book of Occasional Services, 2022.
Lesser Feasts and Fasts, 2022.
The Hymnal, 1982.
Lift Every Voice and Sing, 1993.
Wonder, Love and Praise, 1997.
Voices Found, 2003.
Revised Common Lectionary: Episcopal Edition. Church Publishing, 2007.

Other Manual for Altar Guild and Acolytes

Taylor, B. Don. *The Complete Training Guide for Altar Guilds*. Church Publishing, 1993.
Speer, Roger and Pearson, Sharon Ely. *I Serve at God's Altar*. Church Publishing, 2018.

Priest Manuals

Michno, Dennis. *A Priest's Handbook*. Morehouse, 1998.
Malloy, Patrick. *Celebrating the Eucharist*. Church Publishing, 2007.

Additional Reading

Farwell, James. *The Liturgy Explained*. Morehouse, 2013.
Meyers, Ruth and Mitchell, Leonel. *Praying Shapes Believing: A Theological Commentary on the* Book of Common Prayer. Seabury, 2016.

Two Good Companies for all of your Church Supplies

CM ALMY
133 Ruth Street
Pittsfield, ME 04967
1-800-225-2569
www.almy.com

TREVOR FLOYD & COMPANY
P.O. Box 74
Sussex, NJ 07461
(973) 875-8974
www.trevorfloyd.com

APPENDIX F
GLOSSARY

A

Ablutions:	Ceremonial cleansing of the chalice and paten by the celebrant or deacon at the conclusion of Communion.
Acolyte:	One who assists the celebrant and deacon at the Eucharist (sometimes used for torcher bearer and sometimes called an Altar Server)
Advent Wreath:	Four candles arranged usually with a green wreath, one of which is lighted on the first Sunday in Advent, and one more on each of the following Sundays in Advent. A white candle, the Christ candle, may be placed in the center of the circle and lighted on Christmas Eve, and thereafter during the Christmas season.
Alb	A white, sleeved garment which covers the entire cassock.
Alms Basin:	An offering plate.
Altar:	The Holy Table upon which the Holy Eucharist is celebrated.
Altar Bread:	The wafers or bread used at the Eucharist.
Altar Rail:	A railing in front of the altar at which Communion is often administered
Amice:	A large square, or oblong, garment of white linen or cotton. It is worn about the shoulders, tied with crossed strings under the alb.
Alms Basin:	A large circular vessel of silver, in which are placed the offerings of the congregation

Antependia:	A term to describe the silk or brocade hangings that are placed on the altar, pulpit and lectern
Aumbry:	The wall cabinet in the Sanctuary that contains consecrated bread and wine and holy oils. Also referred to as a 'tabernacle'.

B

Baptistry:	The place where the font is located, sometimes near the entrance of the Church or a place separate from the Church building itself.
Baptismal Towel:	The long, narrow towel which the presider uses to 'dry off' the newly baptized.
Bible Markers:	The silk hangings which decorate the lectern.
Bishop:	The highest order of ordained ministry in the Episcopal Church; the head of the Diocese, elected by the Diocese.
Bishop Coadjutor:	A bishop elected and given jurisdiction to assist and later to succeed the diocesan Bishop.
Bishop Suffragan:	A bishop elected to assist the diocesan bishop, but without jurisdiction or right of succession.
Bishop's Chair:	A special chair in the sanctuary of the Cathedral, reserved for the Diocesan Bishop.
Bread Box:	The small, round, silver 'boxes' with lids which hold the wafers for Holy Eucharist.
Burse:	A square flat case used to hold the corporal and purificator. It is placed on the veiled chalice at the Eucharist.

C

Cassock:	The long usually black garment worn by participants in the liturgy over their "street clothes" and under an alb, cotta, or surplice.

	Sometimes cassocks might be of a different color or have piping to signify a special office.
Cassock-Alb:	Commonly called an alb also, it is a heavier weight long white garment designed to be worn without a cassock.
Cere Cloth:	The protective cloth which goes on the altar between the frontal and the fair linen. This protects the linen of the frontal and the altar from wine spills.
Chalice:	The 'goblet' from which wine is served.
Chalice Veil:	A square covering of silk or brocade used to cover the chalice and paten before and after the Eucharist.
Chancel:	The area which contains the choir pews, the organ, the pulpit, the lectern, and the altar.
Chasuble:	The chief Eucharistic vestment, it is 'poncho-shaped' garment which the presider wears usually wears at Holy Eucharist. It is worn over the alb and stole.
Chimere:	A long garment with arm holes, but without sleeves. It is worn by a bishop over the rochet and may be either red or black.
Chrism	A holy oil consecrated by bishops to be used for ritual anointing at baptisms, confirmations, and ordinations.
Ciborium:	A chalice like cup with a cover, used for the bread at the Eucharist. It may be used in place of the bread box.
Cincture:	A wide flat cloth belt worn around the cassock.
Cope:	A long, elaborate cloak of colored silk or brocade worn by a bishop or priest at festival occasions. It has a clasp at the neck called a morse.

Cotta:	A white garment similar to a surplice, but shorter. Usually worn by choir and acolytes over the cassock.
Corporal	A square cloth of white linen. The sacred vessels are placed upon it at a celebration of the Holy Communion.
Credence Linen	A linen used to cover the credence table.
Credence Table:	The shelf or table on the side of the altar. This table holds the wine and wafers to be consecrated, the lavabo bowl, and the lavabo towel.
Crozier:	A bishop's pastoral staff.
Crucifer:	The cross-bearer in a procession.
Crucifix:	The cross with the figure of Jesus upon it.
Cruets:	The small pitchers which hold wine and water.

D

Dalmatic:	A long squared vestment worn by deacons over their alb and stole
Dean:	The chief of the clergy on the staff of a cathedral; also the head of a seminary.
Diocese:	The see or jurisdiction of a bishop.
Dossal:	A tapestry or curtain which hangs behind the altar.
Dust Cover:	The linen cloth which covers the altar fair linen after the worship service is over. A dust cover is often of a coarser weave of linen than the fair linen. It is simply a dust cover, even though it may be embroidered with crosses.

E

Elements:	The bread, wine, and water which are used at the Eucharist.

Epistle Side:	The right side of the chancel as one faces the altar.
Eucharist:	One of the most ancient names for the Holy Communion; comes from the Greek meaning "thanksgiving."
Eucharistic Vessels:	Any or all of the containers and 'dishes' used for the Eucharist.
Vestments:	The special vestments often worn at a celebration of the Eucharist or Holy Communion: alb, (amice), girdle, stole, (maniple) and chasuble.
Ewer:	The large pitcher which holds water for baptisms. When there is a baptism, the ewer is filled with war, water just before the service, and placed on a small table near the font.

F

Fair Linen:	The principal large white linen cloth which covers the altar, required by rubric.
Flagon:	A large cruet used to hold for large celebrations of the Eucharist
Followers:	The brass 'collars' which fit the tops of the candles to protect against drafts.
Font:	The large basin, often of stone or wood, where baptisms occur.
Frontal:	A full-length hanging for the altar that reaches to the floor.

G

Girdle:	A white cotton or linen rope worn about the waist over the alb. Black girdles are sometimes worn over the cassock. It is also sometimes called a cincture.
Gospel Book:	The book which contains all of the Gospel readings.

Gospel Side: The left side of the chancel as once faces the altar.

H

Hangings: All of the colored silk items that decorate the sanctuary and chancel.

Host   The consecrated bread or wafer at the Holy Communion. The priest's host is larger than the wafers used to communicate the people.

Priest's **Host:**   The large wafer which is held up and broken by the celebrant at the Eucharist.

Hymn Board: The wooden board on the wall of a church which lists the day of the Church season and the hymns for the day.

I

IHS: The first three letters of the name of Jesus in Greek. Also the initial letters of Jesus hominem salvator, Latin for "Jesus the Savior of humankind."

L

Lavabo Bowl: The small silver bowl which is used by the priest for the symbolic washing of hands before celebrating the Eucharist. It is placed on the credence table with the lavabo towel.

Lavabo Towel: The small linen towel on the credence table, next to the lavabo bowl, with which the priest dries their hands after the symbolic washing of hands before celebrating the Eucharist.

Lectern: The podium from which the lessons are read.

Lectionary Book: The book which contains all the Sunday Bible readings for the year. Texts change from Year A to Year B to Year C beginning with the first Sunday in Advent.

Liturgical Colors: The appropriate color for the day according to the Church calendar. It is the color of the hangings and the color of the clergy's vestments. The basic seasonal colors are:

Advent	Blue or Purple
Christmas	White or Gold
Epiphany	Green
Lent	Purple or Unbleached Linen
Easter	White or Gold
Pentecost	Red
Trinity Sunday	White
Sundays After Pentecost	Green
Saints Days	White
Martyrs	Red

Litany Desk: The portable kneeling bench or prayer desk.

M

Maniple: A short band or scarf worn on the left arm of the celebrant at Holy Communion as part of the Eucharistic vestments. Most priests no longer use a maniple.

Mensa: The top of the altar or Holy Table.

Missal: Now known in many churches as the altar book; it contains the services of the Holy Eucharist, the collects, epistles, and gospels.

Missal Stand: The stand or desk upon which the missal rests, sometimes called an altar book stand.

Mitre: The liturgical headdress worn by bishops, symbolizing a tongue of fire descending upon the Apostles. (Also may be spelled Miter)

O

Oblations: The bread and wine brought to the altar at the offertory.

Oblation Table: A table which holds the bread and wine, the 'oblations', which are to be brought forward by members of the congregation during the offertory.

Offertory: The bringing of oblations and alms to the altar.

Office: A service of the Church, other than Holy Eucharist, such as Morning or Evening Prayer.

Office Candles: The candles behind the altar on the retable next to the cross in the sanctuary. These candles, which are lit for all services

Orphrey: An embroidered band on a chasuble or other vestment or hanging.

P

Pall: This word means "covering." It refers to two quite different coverings:

A *pall* is the small, linen covered square of plexiglas which is used to cover the paten and host wafer on a vested chalice.

The *funeral pall is* the large, embroidered silk covering which covers the casket for a funeral.

Paschal Candle: The large, decorated candle which is lit at the Easter Vigil and burns throughout the Easter season to Pentecost. The Paschal candle is also used at baptisms and funerals.

Paten: The plate from which the communion wafers are served.

Pectoral Cross: The large cross worn by bishops.

Piscina: A drain in the sacristy which goes directly to the ground instead of into the sewer system. It is used for the disposal of consecrated

	elements: wine in chalices, bread crumbs on paten, wine rinsed from purificators, and water from Holy Baptism.
Pulpit Fall:	The decorative silk rectangle which hangs from the pulpit.
Purificator:	The small linen square which the ministers of Communion use to wipe the rim of the chalice; acts like a napkin.

R

Reredos:	Usually made of stone or marble, it is the decorated wall behind and above the altar.
Reserved Sacrament:	Consecrated bread and wine, the Body and Blood of Christ, that has not been distributed to communicants in a service of Holy Eucharist, and is kept in an aumbry or tabernacle. A small amount of consecrated bread and wine is often reserved for use by the priest and lay ministers in visitations, or for the sick, dying, or other similar circumstances.
Retable:	A shelf behind the altar, also called a *gradine*.
Rochet:	A long white linen vestment with wide sleeves tied at the wrists, worn by a bishop under a chimere.
Rood:	A cross or crucifix.
Rubric:	A rule or direction in the Book of Common Prayer governing the conduct of liturgies.

S

Sacristy:	A room where preparations are made for the worship service. Sometimes there is one for the Altar Guild and one for the clergy, acolytes and Eucharistic ministers; sometimes there is one large one for all involved in preparation for the liturgy.

Sanctuary: The space inside the altar rail around the altar.

Sanctuary Lamp: A candle in the sanctuary that is constantly lit whenever there is reserved sacrament present in the aumbry or tabernacle.

"The Stack:" See Veiled or Vested Chalice

Stole: A long narrow band of silk worn over the shoulders of the clergy at the Eucharist. It is worn over the alb, and usually matches the color of the hangings.

Superfrontal: A short hanging for the front of the altar. It may be used over a frontal or separately, and it may be made of lace or silk.

Surplice: A white vestment with full flowing sleeves worn over a cassock.

T

Tabernacle: Similar to an aumbry, it is where the reserved sacrament is kept. To distinguish, tabernacles tend to be attached to or immediately behind the altar; whereas an aumbry is separate. Sometimes churches have a tabernacle for the reserved sacrament and an aumbry for holy oils.

Thurible: A vessel for burning incense swung on chains. Sometimes called a censer. The "boat" is the vessel that goes with it to hold the incense.

Tippet: A black scarf, wider than a stole, worn about the neck, with ends hanging down the front. It is worn by the clergy at choir offices.

Tunicle: Similar to a dalmatic though with less ornamentation, it is often worn by crucifers or sub-deacons, when there are three sacred ministers.

V
Vested Chalice: The prepared chalice, covered by a purificator, paten, and burse and veil. Sometimes called "veiled chalice." Affectionately called "the stack."

W
Wafer: The unleavened bread used at the Eucharist.

APPENDIX G
SAMPLE COMMISSIONING

Holy Baptism calls all people to ministry within the Church. A special commissioning of new members or directors of the Altar Guild, while not necessary, is a form of special recognition for the work they do in the congregation. This form may be used following the Nicene Creed at a celebration of the Eucharist or following the Collects in the Daily Office.

Commissioning of Altar Guild Members and Sacristans[1]

Presider / Officiant	Beloved in Christ Jesus, we are all baptized by the one Spirit into one Body, and given gifts for a variety of ministries for the common good. Our purpose now is to commission *these persons* in the Name of God and of this *congregation* (*diocese, parish, community*) to a special ministry to which *they are* called.
Sponsor	I present *these persons* to be admitted to the ministry of *Altar Guild* (*Sacristan, Verger*) in this congregation.
Presider/Officiant	Are *these persons* prepared by a commitment to Christ as Lord, by regular attendance at worship, and by the knowledge of *their* duties, to exercise this ministry to the honor of God, and the well-being of Christ's Church?
Sponsor	I believe they are.

1. Adapted from The Book of Occasional Services (New York: Church Hymnal Corporation, 1994), p 180-185.

Presider / Officiant   You have been called to a ministry in this congregation. Will you, as long as you are engaged in this work, perform it with diligence and faithfully and reverently execute the duties of your ministry to the honor God and the benefit of this community?

Candidate(s)   I will.

Presider / Officiant   Let us pray. *(Silence)*

O God, you accepted the service of Levites in your temple, and your Son was pleased to accept the loving service of friends: Bless the ministry of *these persons* and give *them* your grace, that *they*, caring for the vessels and vestments of your worship and the adornment of your sanctuary, may make the place of your presence glorious, through Jesus Christ, the Great High Priest. Amen.

Presider / Officiant   In the Name of God, and of this *congregation* (*diocese, parish, community*), I commission you [N.] as a *member of the Altar Guild* (*Sacristan, Verger*) of this *parish* [and give you this _____ as a symbol of your ministry].

APPENDIX H
ADDITIONAL PRAYERS

AN ALTAR GUILD PRAYER

Almighty God, grant, we beseech thee, that we may handle holy things with reverence, and perform our work with such faithfulness and devotion that it may rise with acceptance before thee and obtain thy blessing: through Christ our Lord. Amen. [Source unknown]

BEFORE WORSHIP

O Almighty God, who pours out on all who desire it the spirit of grace and of supplication: Deliver us, when we draw near to you, from coldness of heart and wanderings of mind, that with steadfast thoughts and kindled affections we may worship you in spirit and in truth; through Jesus Christ our Lord. Amen. [833]

AFTER WORSHIP

Grant, Almighty God, that the words which we have heard this day with our outward ears, may, through your grace, be so grafted inwardly in our hearts, that they may bring forth in us the fruit of good living, to the honor and praise of your Name; through Jesus Christ our Lord. Amen. [834]

THE NATIONAL ALTAR GUILD ASSOCIATION PRAYER

Written by The Right Reverend E. Don Taylor
Most gracious Father Who has called me Your child to serve in the preparation of Your Altar, so that it may be a suitable place for the offering of Your Body and Blood; Sanctify my life and consecrate my

hands so that I may worthily handle those Sacred Gifts which are being offered to You. As I handle holy things, grant that my whole life may be illuminated and blessed by You, in whose honor I prepare them, and grant that the people who shall be blessed by their use, may find their lives drawn closer to Him Whose Body and Blood is our hope and our strength, Jesus Christ our Lord. Amen.

APPENDIX I

AN ALTAR GUILD HYMN

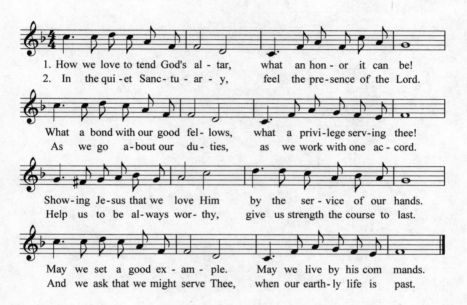

1. How we love to tend God's al - tar, what an hon - or it can be!
2. In the qui - et Sanc - tu - ar - y, feel the pre - sence of the Lord.

What a bond with our good fel - lows, what a privi - lege serv - ing thee!
As we go a - bout our du - ties, as we work with one ac - cord.

Show - ing Je - sus that we love Him by the ser - vice of our hands.
Help us to be al - ways wor - thy, give us strength the course to last.

May we set a good ex - am - ple. May we live by his com - mands.
And we ask that we might serve Thee, when our earth - ly life is past.

Text: Arlene P. Goodenough (1936-2023) for the Diocesan Altar Guild *(Diocese of Long Island)*

Tune: *Erie*, Charles C. Converse (1832-1918)